the biography

tulisa
the biography

Chas Newkey-Burden

JB

JOHN BLAKE

Published by John Blake Publishing Ltd,
3 Bramber Court, 2 Bramber Road,
London W14 9PB, England

www.johnblakepublishing.co.uk

www.facebook.com/Johnblakepub facebook

twitter.com/johnblakepub twitter

First published in paperback in 2012

ISBN: 978 185782 670 8

British Library Cataloguing-in-Publication Data:

A catalogue record for this book is available from the British Library.

Design by www.envydesign.co.uk

Printed and bound in Great Britain by CPI Group (UK) Ltd

1 3 5 7 9 10 8 6 4 2

© Text copyright Chas Newkey-Burden 2012

Papers used by John Blake Publishing are natural, recyclable
products made from wood grown in sustainable forests.
The manufacturing processes conform to the environmental
regulations of the country of origin.

CONTENTS

INTRODUCTION

Back when she was a streetwise north London teenager, Tulisa would get stopped by the police as she walked down the road: they assumed she was up to no good. Nowadays, people stop her in the street to ask for a photograph or an autograph, and to tell her how much they love her. Such has been the spectacular turnaround for a young woman whose past includes self-harm, suicide attempts, drug use and the emotional suffocation that her mother's mental illness caused in the family home.

Forget the colourful sob stories so beloved of *X Factor* contestants: the show's new judge has been to hell and back, and lived to tell the tale. *The X Factor* positions itself as the saviour of those who find fame through it, but Tulisa found her salvation through music many years before she sat down at that famous table alongside Gary Barlow, Kelly Rowland and Louis Walsh.

Tulisa is a much discussed but little understood young woman. She has been described as the 'mother hen' of her band, N-Dubz, but also accused of being 'definitely trouble'. Elsewhere she has been dubbed 'the most famous chav in the UK', 'chav-tastic', 'rough round the edges' and 'a bit of a loose cannon'. People see different qualities in Tulisa: someone nicknamed her the 'pauper's Beyoncé', yet she has also been compared to movie character Jerry Maguire and wartime UK prime minister Winston Churchill. It is a kooky cocktail of comparisons. All these descriptions have at least an element of truth, but none quite do justice to her complicated and fascinating character. Perhaps the least accurate description of her came from a teacher who said in a class that she 'doesn't even come into the equation – she's not going to do anything with her life'. Tulisa has proven that teacher wrong now, but at the time she believed what the teacher had said. She thought she would never amount to anything.

Yet, in keeping with the well-trodden narrative path of the kid written off at school who rises to great success, she has amounted to so much. N-Dubz has won three MOBO awards, released three sensational albums whose combined sales go into the millions and sold out huge arenas. She has also acted in a popular television drama and several films. She is most famous for her place on that 21st-century broadcasting juggernaut, *The X Factor*. The dental veneers she had fitted to her teeth ahead of her first appearance are symbolic: the rough diamond became a polished jewel as she sauntered into the mainstream. We now have the new

Tulisa who, while not disowning her past, is eyeing a new, sophisticated and mature future. 'I like to see myself as sophisticated chav in an expensive tracksuit,' she has said, trying to bring the various strands of her image together into a coherent whole. 'A polite chav, if you like.'

The turnaround began with N-Dubz, which quickly gave her a direction and something to believe in and live for. Writing music became her form of therapy and self-expression as she faced the challenges and pressures her mother's mental illness created. She says that without the band she would have committed suicide. Then N-Dubz brought her riches and a profile that ultimately allowed her to soar to new heights. Although she is fiercely ambitious and undeniably hardworking, she remains suspicious and dismissive of the show-business treadmill and those who jostle for a place on it. 'I find the whole industry quite shallow, poncy, needy,' she said. 'They are the words I'd use for it. It aggravates me. I don't like it. I spend as much time away from it as I can.' She also roundly dismissed the *X Factor* circus, a circus of which she has now become a star attraction.

She joined the circus ostensibly to replace Cheryl Cole, who had departed for a crack at America that proved as ill-fated as it had always seemed ill-judged. Simon Cowell wanted new-girl Tulisa to be 'trouble', nicknaming her thus. Given her chaotic background, she seemed a gamble on Cowell's part. Would she end-up being too much trouble and risk unbalancing his prize show as it entered a new and uncertain era? In the end she was, if anything, a little too mellow. Despite thumping the table angrily on a few occasions, becoming the subject of an investigation by a broadcasting regulator and then getting embroiled in a hellishly ongoing row about a contestant's alleged bullying, Tulisa slotted into the mainstream with surprising ease.

She has squeezed so much into the first 24 years of her life that one wonders what the future holds. In the immediate future, she has a raft of new projects lined-up including a solo album. Her place as an *X Factor* judge seems a sure-fire bet for a few years. She has worked so hard for her fame that she is not about to surrender her place in the spotlight easily. Yet the glamorous lifestyle of her early twenties could scarcely be more different to that of a few years earlier, when she regularly self-harmed, considered suicide and struggled to cope with vicious school bullies and the challenges of her mother's illness. 'Obviously, my past has affected me,' she said in 2011. 'I can't pinpoint how exactly.' What a past it is. Let's go back to the beginning.

CHAPTER ONE

Much has been said of the dramatic transformation Tulisa made to her appearance and image when she signed up to join the *X Factor* judges' panel in 2011 – but that was not the first time she had radically reinvented herself, as all pop artists must do if they hope their fame will endure. The feisty, urban-imaged Tulisa of N-Dubz is significantly different to the Tulisa of her early years a school. In fact, Tula Paulinea Contostavlos was a shy, geeky pupil at the La Sainte Union school, which she attended until she was 12. There, she often stood alone in the playground. She was nearly always too timid to speak during class.

'I'd always be the odd little one out,' she later recalled. She did try to fall in with the in-crowd but kept getting it wrong. As a consequence of this she rarely stayed friends with people for long and tended to drift quietly from group to group. Despite her shy behaviour she was as bright as button and a conscientious student. Her homework was always delivered on time and usually received top marks from her admiring teachers.

X Factor viewers will remember well how she thumped the judges' table as she defiantly explained with a roar how she 'worked my way up from Camden – that's why I'm here today!' She has indeed worked hard – but not entirely as an outsider. Her family actually has an entertainment industry heritage going back generations. Indeed, her mother, Ann Byrne, was a pop star who herself came to prominence through a television reality show. Ann had grown-up in Dublin's southern suburb of Churchtown. She moved to England when she was 15, and was soon keenly chasing musical fame. For Ann, she was to achieve it on *Rising Stars*, which was the BBC's rival to ITV's *New Faces*, which is itself an antecedent of *The X Factor*.

In fact, the musical heritage in Tulisa's family goes back further than her mother. Tulisa's maternal grandfather Tommy Byrne was a singer in Ireland who found fame as a teenage soprano. He won the Feis Ceoil – an Irish musical competition – three times in a row and went on to sing alongside the likes of Val Doonican and the Four Ramblers. Privately, he also sang the Irish folk tune 'Molly Malone' to Tulisa when she was very young. 'That's where I get my music from,' she said. Also, Tulisa's uncles Michael and Brian Byrne formed a band called The Spicelanders which performed at folk clubs, festivals and contests around Ireland. They then joined forces with the hugely talented Donal Lunny and soon merged their two groups – Lunny's had been called The Emmet Folk – to create a new act called Emmet Spiceland. They enjoyed hits in Ireland including 'Báidín Fheidhlimi', 'Down By The Sally Gardens' and 'Mary From Dungloe'. Brian then moved into musical theatre and made appearances in West End musicals. He went on to marry a dancer from the film *Chitty Chitty Bang Bang* called Mavis Ascot. She later choreographed the original *Riverdance* with Michael Flatley and Jean Butler.

By choosing a musical career herself, Tulisa was following in the footsteps of generations of family and has the industry in her blood. So, how just how musical were Tulisa's ancestors? One of her aunties, Ann's sister Moira, paints a picture of a clan in which the very musical, show-business behaviour continued inside the home. 'Everyone in our family was always singing – it was our way of life. As kids we were forever putting on shows for our parents,' she told the *Daily Mail*. Indeed, during Brian's West End stint, the four girls used to perform in the foyer prior to the show. It was there that they were first spotted by an industry figure, a meeting that was to launch their careers. It was the radio presenter Monty Modlin who saw them singing and invited him on to his show. Before long the sisters were performing live in halls around the country, and were also invited on to television shows, including *Rising Stars*. Sometimes they were the warm-up acts for household names such as Jimmy Tarbuck, Les Dennis, Cannon and Ball and Russ Abbot. Mr Dennis was one of those who picked Ann out of the pack. He loved it when she sang 'The Trolley Song', by Judy Garland. During the between-song banter that was all part of the girls' act, Ann stood out as a true wit and mimic. 'She would have us howling with her impressions of Marilyn Monroe,' said Moira.

What fun they had during these musical evenings – but pain was just around the corner for Ann. At the age of 18, her band Jeep began to take off, with hits such as 'Chattanooga Choo Choo'. They would sometimes don US military clothing to perform on a real-life army jeep. It was also around then some of those close to her became troubled by noticeable changes in her behaviour. The first signs of her mental-health issues were appearing, though not in a form that anyone could have properly understood at the time. Her sister Moira said that it was only when Ann entered her twenties that she noticed the issue developing. It was during a trip to Monte Carlo that she particularly began to notice them. 'She went very quiet, very motionless, very thin – but racy. Her body was racing but she was very blank. We knew she was having problems but we didn't have a diagnosis…It was very upsetting to see it and very scary to see it.' Just a week later, the band split up.

In the wake of Jeep's break-up, it was expected that, of all its members, Ann was the most likely to continue building a successful career in music. However, the expected solo success was not to transpire. Instead, there was pain and disappointment in store for Ann as her mental health issues took hold on her life. In 1988, she married Steve 'Plato' Contostavlos, another musician. He was a 'session' musician – a freelance performer available for short-term hire by acts needing such talent. Among those he had played for were the English rock band Mungo Jerry, most famous for their 1970s hit 'In The Summertime'. He also sometimes worked as a barber, in Edgware, north London. This uncertain professional life meant that his income was similarly erratic. However, Plato came from comfortable stock. His father, Spiros, was a diplomat who had worked at the United Nations alongside Kofi Annan and the family owned a five-bedroom house in West Hampstead, as well as a holiday villa in Greece.

Their marriage prompted Ann and Plato to form their own musical outfit for a while, playing alongside Plato's brother Byron. 'They wanted to be rock stars,' explained N-Dubz member Fazer in the band's book *Against All Odds*. Instead, they were to become parents, as our heroine officially enters the story. Within months of Ann marrying Plato, she gave birth to a beautiful baby daughter on 13 July 1988. They named her Tula Paulinea, though she was soon referred to as 'Tulisa' as she grew up as an only child. In Ancient Greek her name means 'the lady herself says', a balance between good and evil. In the 'naughty but nice' image she has developed since maturing from N-Dubz into her *X Factor* role, she partially lives this out.

How much has she fulfilled other potential destinies? There is a growing belief that people's birth order position

– whether they are a first, middle, last or only child – has a considerable influence on their character. Tulisa is an only child, and has said that this meant she was a loner. Historically, there was some stigma about only children, who were a rarity. However, changes in social attitudes – particularly the empowerment of mothers to decide for themselves how many children they wish to have – have seen an increase in the number of families with just one child and therefore also in the acceptance of such children. Only children often have high levels of self-confidence and strong communication skills, due partly to the fact that as they grew up they heard and participated in more adult conversations than they would have done with more children in the household. Tulisa was Plato and Ann's only child together.

She has never stated her opinion on the birth order theories but Tulisa has indicated that she does believe in astrology. She had a tattoo on her body that represented her star sign, Cancer. Characteristics and traits commonly associated with Cancerians by those who believe in astrology have been seen in Tulisa. For instance, her nurturing side which has been seen multiple times, most strikingly in the almost maternal role she has taken with her own mother and also in the way she so effortlessly took to the mentor role in *The X Factor*. However, the often-nostalgic Cancerians are sometimes plagued by fears that bad experiences they have had in the past will repeat in their future. Tulisa is known to be haunted by fears that the hell she went through due to her mother's mental health issues will reappear in her life. She particularly fears that she will succumb to the same illnesses, and has investigated the chances of this happening, as we shall see.

Long before that fear gripped her, Tulisa grew up aware of and often submerged in the musical and theatrical atmosphere of the elder members of her family. As we have seen, her grandfather sang Irish folk songs to her. She also often heard the sound of 1940s American music and it was this that began to inform both her interest in becoming a vocalist and, ultimately, her vocal style. 'I don't really listen to it any more but I'm sure that some of my vocal sound probably comes from training my voice from young to 40s music so it has that powerful vibe to it,' she later said. Many of Britain's recently successful female singers grew up listening to the music that influenced their sound. Adele, for instance, heard the sounds of Ella Fitzgerald, Nina Simone, Louis Armstrong and Bob Dylan as a child. As for the late, great Amy Winehouse, both sides of her family are steeped in music for generations, so the sounds of jazz and blues were the soundtrack to her formative years as well. The soundtrack of one's youth clearly has an effect. As Tulisa said in one of the first interviews N-Dubz ever gave: 'I didn't get no [vocal] training, I must have grown up listening to music.'

Music brought Tulisa moments of happiness that she needed as her mother's mental health issues increasingly became part of her life. She will always remember the terrifying day when she was just five years of age and she watched her mother taken away to a hospital to be sectioned. Now, she understands what happened and also the seriousness of someone being placed under psychiatric care, but at the time she only knew something very upsetting had happened. 'My parents were arguing and I remember the police and ambulance lights flashing outside as my mum was taken away to the Royal Free Hospital in Hampstead, North London,' she told the *Daily Mail*, looking back. 'I knew something was wrong because everyone around me was upset but I didn't understand what was actually going on.'

The trauma continued when Tulisa next saw her mother, and realised afresh that there was something seriously wrong with her. However, within weeks of that visit it seemed that everything was rosy again. 'I visited her in hospital and she seemed distant, not like my mum at all,' said Tulisa. 'But she came back home after a few weeks and life seemed to get back to normal.' It did not seem that way for long. Soon, Ann's mental health issues began to cause problems for the family again. It was claimed that, for instance, Plato once found Ann trying to feed young Tulisa raw eggs. Tulisa was reportedly sitting at the table saying, 'Please, Mummy, don't. They're raw.' The danger of this moment is clear, but it would soon be upstaged by ever more terrifying turns of events. Tulisa, as an only child, began to feel 'suffocated' in the family home due to the issues and would go on to behave troublingly, even resorting to self-harm.

The problems underlying this were both serious and deep-rooted. Ann had been suffering from a schizoaffective disorder since before Tulisa's birth. Its symptoms are a cruel combination of those of schizophrenia and bipolar disorder: hallucinations, delusions and wild mood swings from the pits of despair to manic elation. In Ann's case, she would have what Tulisa has described as 'episodes'. They would, she wrote, 'bubble up during the year and she'd have to go into hospital for one to four months'. The episodes included her hearing voices, severe mood swings, periods of intense paranoia and potent emotions. Naturally, Ann's condition was an enormous strain on Tulisa throughout her childhood; at times it made life almost unbearable for her. She tried to be as loving and supportive as she could, but as she wrote it was extremely 'hard watching her suffer'. Even while discussing this most upsetting of issues, she is keen to emphasise that her mother is 'a beautiful, kind person' and her 'idol'. Ann's older sister – and former Jeep co-member – Louise sometimes stepped in to help, inviting Tulisa to go and stay with her when the going got tough. One such intervention was key, as we shall see.

Significantly, given the road Tulisa would later take, Ann's behaviour was a factor in turning her daughter into more of a street girl. She recalled how the 'whole…worry' of her mother's mood swings meant she would often avoid being in the house altogether. 'I never wanted to go home and be around that,' she wrote. This was not just for her own sake but also for her mother's. 'It made me sad, so I would stay out and try not to worry her with my problems.' Even when trained experts attempted to help,

Tulisa felt that their interventions were unsuccessful. 'The doctors didn't seem to be able to stabilise my mother's moods and I felt myself being dragged further and further down by the environment I was forced to live in,' she said in 2010. 'Music and my dream of becoming a success was all that kept me going through those very dark times.'

Her father, too, suffered greatly, so it was not a huge surprise when Plato eventually lost patience with the situation and left the family home. However, it made for some difficult times between father and daughter. He had met a new woman, called Mel. Plato and Mel had first met in the late 1990s. Plato wooed her using an unconventional gambit: 'If you agreed to date me, and we dated for a year, would you marry me?' When he told Tulisa that he was leaving Ann, it was the hardest conversation they had ever had. His daughter, who had already been through so much, was distraught. 'I could see how sad she looked but I had just had enough,' he said. 'I just needed my own space.' For Ann, and therefore for Tulisa, this parting had severe consequences. 'My dad left home and it triggered one of her episodes,' said Tulisa of her mother's response. 'One minute she'd look all mournful as if someone had died, the next she'd be angry and aggressive, smashing cupboards and shouting. I wasn't allowed to turn on the TV because she thought it might harm us – the same with the hot water.'

Life was becoming genuinely intolerable for Tulisa. She was not even 10 years of age and yet was having to face the most difficult of experiences. To watch, at the age of nine, one's parents split was enough in itself. However, she had also seen her mother sectioned to psychiatric care and had witnessed at first hand the erratic behaviour that had led to that move. 'It was impossible to have a conversation with my mum because she'd drift off into her own little world, but at the same time she didn't want me to go out and leave her so I couldn't even escape to a friend's house. I was like a prisoner in the flat with her. Inevitably, she went into hospital again and I stayed with my mum's older sister, Louise. She had children of her own and it was felt she was more able to look after a young girl.' Tulisa spoke to *The Sunday Times* about what life was like for her in the aftermath of her parents' divorce. 'Me and my mum spent a year in a one-bed council flat,' she said. 'There was no shower – we'd have to run across the hall, so it was far from glamorous. Don't get me wrong, my dad did his utmost to support me. He worked, but he was never rich. Most days, I would live off £3.'

Around the same time, Tulisa changed her appearance, as she began to become aware of the attraction of boys. 'I grew out my horrible fringe and got my ears pierced, pulled my hair back off my face, put on a shorter skirt and undid my top button – and that was it: I found I got a lot more male attention,' she said. Not that her rebellious ways could conceal the sweet, frightened girl underneath it all. Nor could it entirely destroy her already notable spirit. Take, for instance, the impression young Tulisa first made on her stepmother, Mel. 'She was a lovely little girl,' Mel told the *Daily Mail*. 'I remember her telling jokes, mimicking members of her family. She was a happy-go-lucky character.'

Tulisa remains a fine mimic to this day. 'There didn't seem to be any ill-feeling about me being in her father's life,' said Mel. 'They were very close and she appeared happy to be around him, happy to be in his presence. You could see there was definitely a bond there – she adored her father. She was polite and well-mannered – very much so.' Tulisa's father and his new wife took her on day trips to the zoo and once for a weekend holiday in Wales. She won a singing competition at a Butlins holiday camp, performing Laura Branigan's hit song 'Gloria' to great acclaim.

Plato wanted to gain joint custody of Tulisa, who he was convinced would be better off with him. So he encouraged Mel to marry him so his legal case for custody would be stronger. 'He put the squeeze on me and said it would help his cause to have a stable environment for Tulisa to come to every weekend,' Mel told the *Daily Mail*. 'I felt I was being rushed into things, that there had been no time for the relationship to develop properly. I was only 25. But my own father had been schizophrenic and I understood the effects of mental illness on a child. I went along with it, despite huge doubts.' She said Plato told her the day after the wedding that she would have to return to work straightaway, as she needed to bring income into the home because he 'wasn't built for nine-to-five.' His bid for joint custody failed, to his devastation, said Mel.

Meanwhile, Ann's problems continued. On one occasion, she phoned Plato and Mel to inform them that the 'devil is climbing up the walls'. Tulisa was in the house with Ann at the time and could be heard crying in the background as her mother broke down over the phone. Ann was returned to the Royal Free Hospital in Hampstead but nobody knew where Tulisa was. It transpired that, in a moment of awful neglect, she had been left crying on the doorstep by the social services staff who had taken Ann to hospital. At just 10 years of age Tulisa was more alone and vulnerable than ever. She walked to the local pub where the landlord – who knew the family – took her in and called Tulisa's aunt to come and collect her.

Tulisa had always done her best to smile through the turmoil but in the wake of that incident the brave face she tried to put on things was rarely seen. She would disappear, and then phone up asking to be collected from places as far away as Bristol. Indeed, so depressed did she become that she started to self-harm. It started when she began to cut her own arms with scissors. This became an increasingly grave problem. Before long these were not just small nicks in her arms: she was, in her own words 'slicing up my arms'. She also used to smash her head against the wall at night with sheer frustration at her life. This was not the behaviour of a girl who was entirely happy-go-lucky. She could not have known then what joys and riches would come to her later in life. Not least because in the immediate future life was about to throw more painful trials her way. They say your schooldays are the happiest of your life. Well, don't try telling Tulisa that. The loneliness she had felt at La Sainte Union was to be replaced by some horrific times at her next educational establishment. Indeed, after what she went through in the latter years of her schooling she would argue that schooldays can often be the very worst days of your life.

CHAPTER
TWO

When she was 12 years old, Tulisa enrolled in Haverstock School in Camden. She describes it as a place quite out of the ordinary. Indeed, her immediate memories of the place are quite shocking. 'We used to have police outside every day,' she told *The Sunday Times*. 'Whoever did what they did out of that school, bloody well done to them, because when I was there, it was horrific.' Former pupils of the school include Labour leader Ed Miliband and 1980s football star John Barnes. However, the most important pupils in Tulisa's mind were two who were there at the time: her cousin Dino and his best friend Richard Rawson, who are now better known as Dappy and Fazer of N-Dubz. They had first met at karate lessons when they were around the age of seven. It has become an enduring friendship. The day before she started at Haverstock, it was Dappy who took her clothes shopping, so she would fit in better. Without an elder sibling to look up to in the style stakes, Tulisa had been clothed by her mother up until then.

It was the first makeover of Tulisa's life, though certainly not the last. First, they went to a couple of footwear stores, and emerged with a pair of Nike trainers. They then drifted through other clothes stores as they assembled a new outfit for Tulisa: a baseball jacket, a jumper from Gap and a pair of Nike tracksuit bottoms. What a fun day it was, as Dappy helped her choose the right gear. She really looked up to her cousin, who is a year older than her and had a sort of sibling role from early in their lives. The Dappy-commissioned makeover was complete when a female friend of his helped Tulisa slick her hair back. Having given Tulisa a new look for her new school, he then set to work on her etiquette. He encouraged her to play it a bit more cool but also to be more open than she had been prior to then. He wanted her to come out of her shell at Haverstock and to be accepted and popular, much like he was.

For the first eight months there she was so happy. She enjoyed the co-educational atmosphere and tried to carry herself with some of the swagger of her popular cousin Dappy. One day while Tulisa was taking a PE class a girl swiped her tracksuit bottoms from where she had left them in the changing room. Tulisa believed that the theft was motivated by the fact that the bottoms actually belonged to her hugely popular cousin. She laughed the incident off and borrowed another pair from a friend. If anything, she enjoyed the reflected glory of being the cousin of such a popular pupil. 'I thought it was so cool,' she said. 'I was going there as Dappy's cousin. That made me cool. Automatically, the whole popular crowd embraced me. All the girls wanted to know me, because they all fancied Dappy. It was great.' Soon, she was hanging out with the 'cool' kids and became one of the school's more popular pupils. She became confident around boys and also befriended some teenagers from local estates who she would never have previously had the confidence to approach and attempt to befriend. She also began to drink alcohol and smoke cannabis – such behaviour was 'a standard thing for everyone' at the school, she later wrote. She convinced older girls to go into the shop for her and buy her some alcohol. Vodka, cider and beer were her usual tipples. She said she got 'absolutely smashed' for the first time as a 12-year-old and was soon 'getting messy' each weekend, including at under-18s rave parties.

It was a welcome source of escapism for a girl who, lest we forget, was still going through hell at home. 'When I was 12 I wanted to have fun,' she said, looking back later. 'I didn't want to go back to the one-bedroom council flat, crying myself to sleep at night. I became a lot gobbier and had my first boyfriend.' Plenty of her classmates were even having sex, she said.

Tulisa claimed she knew for a fact that pupils were having sex 'in the toilets at the age of 12 in break time'. Soon, such behaviour would provoke tensions and suspicions that would hurt Tulisa. Meanwhile, she was more interested in getting out of her head. Given the history of mental illness in her family, it was rather dangerous for Tulisa to experiment so enthusiastically with a mind-altering drug such as cannabis. Indeed, the very same issues that pushed her towards the drug also meant she should have avoided it. Episodes of users, particularly the young, developing emotional issues as a result of cannabis-use – particularly the stronger modern forms such as skunk – are reasonably commonplace. After a while, she began to have intense panic attacks, complete with terrifying heart palpitations. One day the attack was so bad that she collapsed and started to froth at the mouth before passing out. The next thing Tulisa knew she was coming-to in the back of an ambulance. This terrifying moment drew a line in the sand as far as she was concerned. She has not taken cannabis since.

However, other parts of her newfound confidence and rebellious behaviour continued. The quiet, studious girl of her earlier years was replaced by someone at ease with what she saw as the disrespectful and lazy kids at Haverstock. She has recalled how plenty of the pupils did next to no work, as they were too busy 'screaming at each other and cussing the teachers'. She had never seen the like of this before, but she was so keen to be accepted by her peers that she joined in with this misbehaviour. She estimates that in the 18 months she spent at Haverstock she did little more than two days' worth of actual schoolwork. Her memories of the place no doubt seem accurate to her but how fair they actually are to the school they are is open to question. The school authorities would certainly prefer to paint a more positive picture of the establishment. Dappy has also spoken disparagingly of the school, saying, 'I ain't gonna big up no teachers because it didn't feel like none of them gave a damn about me' and saying it 'gave out no positivity'. Tulisa's favourite moments at school included drama classes and – surprisingly – school dinners. She has always enjoyed the food that most kids dread. She also fondly remembers a school outing to the Natural History Museum in Kensington. She had been obsessed with dinosaurs since watching the movie blockbuster *Jurassic Park*, so she lapped up the chance to study their story at the museum.

There is no doubt Tulisa often misbehaved and slacked, though, and she looks back at this as a 'negative way of blending in'. But some real personal negativity for Tulisa is just about to enter our story. Eight months after she first arrived at Haverstock, she began to be targeted by bullies. A brutal chapter in her school life started with a confrontation between Tulisa and a highly aggressive girl who had been led to believe Tulisa had been bitching about her. In a flash, Tulisa found herself facing more aggression than she had ever encountered before. The girl was face-to-face with Tulisa and screaming abuse at her, while brandishing a pencil and threatening to 'stab' her with it. In an instant, eight months of happiness and fun seemed to disappear as she faced a terrifying, threatening verbal onslaught. However, if Tulisa thought she had tasted a new low, there was to be plenty more where that came from. A process began of fellow pupils wrongly accusing Tulisa of speaking about them in derogatory terms and then attacking her for it either verbally or physically or both. Lots of these rumours concerned Tulisa having sex with boys who were already in relationships. Their girlfriends would naturally be furious and would confront her about the alleged liaison. Words and sometimes shoves or worse would be exchanged. The added hurt for Tulisa was that these rumours were always untrue – she had not slept with any guys at this stage. As she learned, the truth mattered as much in the unforgiving atmosphere of school as it does in the wild west of some celebrity magazines.

Again, Tulisa's good looks and head-turning chest were behind much of this treatment. Girls became jealous and suspicious of her. Although most of the suspicions were unfounded, it was true that she was turning lots of young male heads. When people realised that Tulisa was often being asked out for dates by the most popular guys, a new raft of rumours would be launched to try and dissuade such advances. To make matters worse, just when she needed friends most Tulisa found that some of the people she considered in that category were not worthy of being called friends. She felt alone, frightened and cornered. After some months of this cycle of behaviour Tulisa decided she had to deal with the issue and the person she believed to be at the centre of the rumour-spreading. She confronted the girl and soon a heated argument broke out. Then the girl lost her rag and began punching her in the face. What Tulisa had not realised was that the girl was a victim of bullying as well. So patience for both girls was at a premium as they fought each other. By the time it was over Tulisa had a split lip and was bleeding from her face. Although she insisted in *Against All Odds* that she had landed some damaging blows to her opponent, she added that the wounds she inflicted were all hidden by her hair.

However, as far as the rest of the school was concerned, Tulisa had lost the fight and was a 'pussy'. As her opponent was not a tough girl, this perception was dangerous as it made Tulisa seem vulnerable and weak – and therefore a target for any bully who fancied an easy ride. The problems escalated from there – with enormous seriousness. 'I was always outnumbered,' she said. 'By the time I was 15, to go to my friend's house in Kentish Town, I used to walk around with a baseball bat or a knife on me, because of the fear of being attacked by 15 girls. This was no joke. They would get a bottle, smash it on the floor and happily stab it in your face. I didn't want to hurt anyone, but it was my way of sticking up for myself. It was a dangerous cycle to be in.' A dangerous cycle indeed. Tulisa said that the beatings she received were always severe and left her in a shocking condition: 'Black eyes, bust lip, bottle over the head.' She added: 'By this time, I couldn't go to school because I'd get beaten up.' Why did she not report all this to the police, she was asked. 'No, you wouldn't tell the police,' she explained. 'It was against the code of street law. You couldn't be a grass.'

Instead, she had to be creative and fast-thinking to find a way out of this brutal cycle of violence she seemed stuck in. She could not, she felt, call on the police to protect her. So she turned to a different kind of authority and courted the protection of the circle of people she considered to be the toughest in the neighbourhood. Her courtship was successful. 'My way of getting out of things was getting in with this really hard crowd – the hardest of the hardest in the area,' she said. 'We were a wild bunch of girls, but I was content being protected.' Finally, she had found a way to stem the tidal wave of violent bullying she had been facing in recent months. Still, she remained vigilant. Sometimes, she later admitted, she would carry a weapon for her own protection. 'I had to walk down the road with a baseball bat in my pocket,' she told the *Radio Times*. 'I didn't end up having to use the bat, but I did have to punch people back.' Arming herself was not a step taken lightly; rather, it was a reaction to some horrific and detailed threats. 'This was a time when people were saying, "We're going to come down with 20 people and put you in hospital".'

Although the approval and resultant protection Tulisa received from her new friends brought great relief for her, by choosing to run with such a tough and unruly crowd she realised she had to quickly start to behave in kind in order to stay in with them. Therefore, this new association of hers sent her further off the rails in terms of behaviour. 'Yeah, we did do naughty things,' she said. What, specifically? 'We did pinch a couple of handbags and get into fights. I wasn't part of a girl gang, though. We were just a group of troublesome chicks. Obviously, we were consuming so much weed and alcohol, we were going loopy anyway.' She later expressed regret for the stolen bags. 'I nicked a couple of handbags and I'm deeply unhappy I did that,' she told *Now* magazine. 'But it was done to give myself power. I was vulnerable, I had no self-worth and I'd do anything to get some attention. So to those people I would say sorry.'

There is something almost moving about Tulisa's claim that some of her misbehaviour as a teenager came not from an inherent nature of hers, but from the neighbourhood she grew up in and then out of a desire for protection from bullies. That said, she has to take responsibility for what she did and must not be allowed to spin herself entirely out of the blame for her actions. Plenty of youngsters have gone through bullying experiences as children but few of them turn to theft as a way out of it. While expressing sorrow to her victims, she also says she would not change anything else about her childhood. As far as Tulisa is concerned, everything she has been through has made her the person she is today. 'There's really nothing else for me to feel ashamed about,' she said, during the same interview in which she expressed regret for the thefts. One senses that she is conflicted in her feelings: on the one hand she feels 'deeply unhappy' for some of what she did, and offers apologies to her victims; on the other hand she says that overall she has nothing to feel ashamed about.

In time, she moved schools and enrolled at Quintin Kynaston, in Marlborough Hill, near Swiss Cottage. She arrived there a different Tulisa to the one that had last enrolled at a new school. This time, she was ready and on the lookout for trouble. Never again was she going to allow herself to be pushed around at school. Educationally, she has since written, 'there was really no point me being there' as she had no interest in learning. Only one teacher – called Miss Shield – had any influence on her. Indeed, Miss Shield had a big influence on her life. When Tulisa bunked off school she would find the teacher on her doorstep, encouraging her to return to school. It was Miss Shield who saw the beautiful gem inside the tough and ugly front that Tulisa felt forced to put up in life. Few other adults in her life managed that. Tulisa and Dappy have both spoken out about education, encouraging their fans to work at school. Indeed, Tulisa has even declared herself in favour of a return to more old-fashioned discipline in today's schools. She believes that if teachers were once more allowed to give pupils a 'cane or a wallop' then society would benefit.

The bullying she worked so hard to overcome had originally been dominated by suggestions and perceptions of her as a sexually active teenager. However, as we have seen, such perceptions were for a long while far wide of the mark. That 'while' ended when Tulisa first had sex with a boy when she was 14 years of age. Despite being two years below the age of consent when she lost her virginity, she now considers that she was in one sense a late, rather than early, starter. 'I was about to turn 15,' she told *The Sunday Times*, looking back on this rite of passage. 'I was one of the lucky ones to keep my virginity for as long as I did.' It seems that the hurried, precocious pace at which Tulisa lost her virginity was shared by most of those around her. 'It's the environment you're from, it becomes normal,' she said. 'Everyone around me had lost it. We were too mature for our age. We were doing things we shouldn't. We shouldn't have been drinking or smoking weed. The first time I went to an over-21s night, I was 13 years old.'

A sense of the circumstances of her first love-making can perhaps be gained by a statement she made much later in life, discussing the sexual politics of young people in the 21st century. It is a sharp, at times weary, analysis of how sexuality for young people has changed. 'This generation is really effed up,' she said, laying down her feeling from the start. 'Chivalry's gone because guys don't have to wait for sex any more. There's so much more booty available than in the old days, when you'd meet someone and settle down quickly. Now everyone has such high expectations. Everyone thinks they can do better, and girls are so desperate for a guy, they've had to fall into the routine. If you want a guy, you've got to shag him.' The interviewer she was speaking to noted that she ended with a sigh. Could that sigh indicate that she was speaking of herself and her own experiences? Did she sometimes sleep with guys because she felt she had to, rather than just because she wanted to?

Certainly, she had many negative experiences with guys before finding happiness. As if there was not enough pain for her at home and at school, she experienced more hardship when she began dating boys. She said that her first 'proper boyfriend' – who followed in the footsteps of a boy called Carlos who she had dated less seriously for 12 months – was violent and abusive towards her. He was a handsome, older man and at first Tulisa was delighted to have won his favour. She had lied about her age to impress him. She was so excited when she would get to stay overnight at his pad. The relationship became a living hell for her though. He routinely and openly cheated on her. He hurled degrading insults at Tulisa, too. He told her she was ugly and worthless. On occasions, he even locked her in the bathroom when he left the house, in an extreme instance of controlling behaviour. Astonishingly, though in a sense typically of Tulisa, later in life she was able to take an understanding look at this man who was so unpleasant to her. She knew he had suffered a 'very tough upbringing' himself and that he was a little lost and in need of help. While she regrets that it was her who faced the backlash of his issues, she understood what had prompted them. She even wrote that she was pleased he had subsequently found help and confronted many of his demons. It takes a mature and forgiving nature to be able to view him that way. That said, she too will have benefited from the serene view she was able to take of the issue.

Back in the thick of it, though, it had been tough for her. The hurt took on a new dimension when the boyfriend broke off the relationship. Tulisa might have been relieved to have escaped the clutches of such an abusive figure. However, at the time she was just hurt and humiliated to watch him run off with another girl. She stopped eating and lost a stone-and-a-half in weight. She also became interested in witchcraft and Tarot cards, as her imagination became ever darker. She remembers trying an Ouija board, and becoming convinced she had 'brought something bad out', as well as believing that her at times ghastly dreams foreshadowed real-life tragedies. She was pulled from this darkness by the light of religion. In her dreams, Mother Mary spoke to her and assured Tulisa that she was watching over her. The female saint was not the only religious icon that 'spoke' to Tulisa in her sleep. Soon, Tulisa began to pray and soon felt the dark and negative energy lessen.

Before she truly stepped into the light, her self-harming escalated and she then went a step further: by attempting suicide on two occasions. The first time she tore into her mother's extensive medication collection and swallowed handfuls of all manner of pills. They quickly took hold of her and she began vomiting violently. It was fortunate her body rejected the lethal concoction of pills she had forced on it, otherwise she would probably have died there and then. Instead, she lived to cry another day. The second suicide attempt came soon afterwards as she battled the pain and humiliation of both the break-up and the relationship that preceded it. This time she moved from her usual self-harming to an all-out attack on her wrists. Quickly she lost her resolve to end her life and realised with panic what was at stake. She grabbed a towel and held it tightly against the cuts. As she sat there in tears, desperately trying to stop the flow of blood, she thanked her lucky stars that she had not torn into crucial veins. It had been a very lucky escape for her; a life-saving one. A single extra slash with the knife just a few millimetres away from those she had made might have ended her life in seconds.

'I know it was a classic cry for help and I decided I had to take myself out of the environment I'd been living in,' she said later, during an interview with the *Daily Mail*. 'So I went to stay with my dad, who also lived in North London. My dad knew what I'd been going through but I'd always chosen to live with my mum. Despite everything, I wanted to be there for her.' Turning to how she felt about her father's physical absence, she was understanding in tone. 'I know my dad felt terrible for what I'd been through but he got really emotional and admitted that he just couldn't stand the constant ups and downs of [my mum's] mood swings and the paranoia any more, which is why he left. Her mood swings were affecting him and making him so depressed he was becoming a different person. I totally understood how it had driven him to the brink and I know that he's sorry he left me to deal with it for all those years.'

Tulisa had not only shocked her father with her suicide attempt – she had also shocked herself. This was something akin to a 'rock-bottom' for her. If her story were a movie script, at this stage Tulisa would have reached a full epiphany. She would immediately have embarked on a positive life, with all her negative behaviour consigned to the past. However, the rough and tumble of real life is rarely so neatly plotted. Instead, she embarked on 12 months of trying to make up for her bad experience with a succession of guys. She still craved real love from a man and was therefore easy prey for guys whose smooth talking was less than sincere. Tulisa was so keen for her buttons to be pressed and there was never any shortage of men happy to press them. They would say the right things about commitment and love, get what they wanted from her and disappear into the night. To paraphrase a song she would later sing with N-Dubz, it did not take much for her to believe every word of their sweet stories.

It was not as if she even always enjoyed the sexual experiences themselves. She admits she would often cry afterwards. More than anything, Tulisa just wanted a cuddle and some kind words. For a while, the sex and subsequent desertion was a price worth paying for those moments of tenderness. Ultimately, the cycle became too painful and she was forced to take a clear-eyed look at what was happening. Soon, she would find a man who treated her more as she deserved to be treated. It would be a major turning point in her life. However, by this stage she had a new love in her life that any man would have to learn to share her attention and affection with. One that would bring her much excitement, joy and hope. A lover that would take her round the world and make her famous. Like many of her ancestors, Tulisa had fallen in love with music. She had also developed a taste for fame that she would spend the years ahead trying to quench. There were plenty more twists and turns to come in her life, but at this stage, Tulisa was finally on the up.

CHAPTER
THREE

In a sense, the band we now know as N-Dubz first got together in 1999, the fateful day when Dappy and Fazer approached Tulisa – who was then just 11 years of age – and asked her to come to a recording studio with them to put together a track. They had gained access to a recording studio thanks to the generous support of Dappy's father Byron – who would become the very heartbeat of the band's early years. He had bought a small recording studio in Dollis Hill, north-west London, acquiring it with the proceeds from his various musical ventures. He became keen to encourage his son Dappy and his friend Fazer to get involved with music. This was, initially, as much as anything to keep them out of trouble. Cynics might say that in Dappy's case at least this was a failed mission. However, one cannot know how he might have strayed without music and the fame that eventually came with it.

Indeed, in the light of some of his childhood experiences, the ever-controversial Dappy has risen to become little short of a shining beacon.

Back in the day, Dappy and Fazer had already messed around in the studio and in their bedrooms at home by the time they approached Tulisa with their big idea. They were enjoying the sounds that were coming together but they had increasingly realised they needed something extra – proper vocals. Tulisa's love of music and performance in general had been growing steadily for years. When she was 11 she appeared in a school production of *Bugsy Malone*. She had being given the role of the female lead, Tallulah, and duly sang the song 'My Name Is Tallulah'. (In later years she would attempt an on-stage gag about this, by singing the '2011 version' called 'My Name Is Tulisa'. The young audiences did not always appreciate the joke.)

Securing that part after her audition and then performing in the production itself gave her enormous confidence as a singer. She clashed with the singing teacher she was given at secondary school. 'I remember hating those lessons because she made me sing like a choir girl,' said Tulisa. 'I just wanted to put some soul into it. She didn't really like me!' Many of her schoolmates did like Tulisa's singing, though. 'At break time people would just crowd around me and I would sit and sing songs people requested,' she wrote. 'It was just T singing time.' During these times her confidence began to soar. 'I truly believed in my heart of hearts that I would be the world's biggest superstar,' she said.

So, along came Dappy and Fazer to ask Tulisa if she would fill their musical void. Her response? A walloping great 'no'. She felt that she wanted to be a solo artist, not help them pursue their dream of forming a band. It was a rather abrupt and perfunctory rejection, by all accounts. Later, she acknowledged she had been 'all snooty' about it. That might have been that, as far as the chances of the trio ever becoming a band was concerned. The boys turned their attention instead to another girl they knew from school. They asked if she would lay down some vocals in the studio, and when she said yes that seemed to seal the deal. However, the singer didn't work out and the boys enlisted Byron to have another crack at convincing Tulisa to join them. He offered Tulisa a £20 note to help convince her. Showing early signs of her confidence in negotiation, she turned it down. He then offered her a 'pinky' – a £50 note – and she finally agreed to join the boys in the studio.

When she got there, she discovered a scene that was less musical and more comical. No wonder Dappy thought she seemed 'aloof'. Fazer and Dappy were playing, as best they could, various instruments including the keyboard. They also twiddled with some of the production buttons that adorned the studio equipment. Their knowledge and ability might not have been sky-high but they were full of passion and enthusiasm. She hoped these qualities would win out, and she was willing to give it a go. She had nothing to lose, after all. Though her first attempts at vocals sounded a little nasal and 'childish' to Dappy, she quickly began to improve. Eventually, after a period in which 'trial and error' sprang easily to mind, they had a rough recording of their first track, which the two boys had been working on. Donna Dee, a music producer who worked with them in the early days, said they created the song 'in a matter of days'. Its title was 'What Is This World Coming To?' A strange choice of title for a teenage urban track, perhaps. It reads more as the headline of a despairing *Daily Mail* leader comment than that of a youthful, urban pop song. Dappy, looking back, said he was 'embarrassed to even say that name'. (It had originally been called 'What Is The World Coming To, We Don't Give A Fuck'.) It didn't matter, though – they had their first song, and they had taken a small but mighty step towards the stardom that would come their way in years ahead. For now, Tulisa said that the song was a little silly, and were it to surface publicly now, people would 'crack up'. Let's hope it does, then.

However, she added, 'I was an 11-year-old with a song – no matter how crap it was!' With a song to their name, the trio decided to give their act a name. Tulisa's suggestion for the band name was Boom Crew. Dappy was not convinced: in fact, Tulisa recalls him 'pissing himself' laughing at her suggestion, which she now concedes was 'corny'. Again, it sounds more like the name a middle-aged man would imagine for an urban act, rather than one that kids themselves would dream up. Instead, they came up with a better one. They reasoned that despite being young, they had 'rinsed it' in the studio. Therefore, they came-up with the name Likkle Rinsers Crew. With a song and a band name created, it was official – Tulisa was in a band! They looked to the future. Naturally, given the nature of the three personalities involved, the focus was not always keen. The three would muck about and Fazer even remembers Tulisa scrapping with some of his friends. At first, the ratio of horseplay to actual music work was close to evenly split. However, as time went on Tulisa and her band-mates became increasingly serious about the music. They still mucked about a bit, naturally. Still do to this day, in fact. The personalities involved make that an inevitability.

Soon, as the band developed, each member took on their own place within the collective. Dappy, as his personality would inevitably dictate, became the focal point of attention and the de facto frontman. He is a young man born for the limelight, a kind of urban combination of Robbie Williams and Johnny Rotten, with a perhaps unintentional dash of Ali G thrown in for good measure. Fazer was described by Tulisa as more like the American rapper and producer Timbaland – a mellow, more retiring yet no less significant figure. He enjoyed playing with guitars and pianos in the early days, and sometimes threw some body-popping moves around. But what of Tulisa? She describes herself as a combination of the natures of her two male band-mates. At times she is as much of an attention-junkie as Dappy, yet she can also be the shyer figure like Fazer. The different characters appeal to different fans. Indeed, Fazer has said that the band is not unlike the Spice Girls – we all have our favourite member. She is also a maternal figure within the band and admits that she sometimes feels she is not just managing their careers but their lives in general. Not that she is a saint. 'I always tell T that there's more work to do,' said Dappy. 'She sometimes goes on like we've done enough and can have a little break.'

Luckily, they had a real-life guardian angel looking over them in the early days, to point them back in the right direction. Always overseeing them was their mentor Byron, or 'B' as they took to calling him. If anyone wanted an example of someone who mentored young musicians with attention, wisdom and love, then they could not have done better than watching B work with the three youngsters. Fazer believed that it was B's disappointment at not fully realising his own musical dreams that drove him to work so carefully and supportively with them. Indeed, B's mentor role went beyond musical matters. He offered them advice and wisdom for their lives in general. Often, it was only later that they realised just how useful and true his tips and thoughts had been. For instance, he warned Fazer that 'vampires' would attach themselves to him once he became famous. This was not just a warning – he also taught the youngster how to recognise such predatory and fake individuals before they got a grip on him.

Tulisa meanwhile has painted a picture of B that suggests he was hard man with a big heart – an attractive and particularly effective combination. For instance, she recalled, if he ever caught whiff that one of the band was indulging in a moment of self-pity he would come down hard on them. 'He was a very harsh man,' she said. Indeed, her stepmother Mel claims she once heard B telling a 13-year-old Tulisa that she needed to lose weight. 'Byron told her she was fat,' she said. 'She was only 13. He said no one wanted to see a fat person on stage. It was so inappropriate.' Naturally, during the long periods of hard work that come before any act 'makes it', there are always moments when individuals concerned will begin to doubt whether it will ever happen for them. Self-pity and crippling doubts are indeed huge enemies of any aspiring artist. Therefore, B's no-nonsense response to any hint of them was in many ways his greatest gift to the band. To be clear, he was not a tough mentor in the style of, say, Joseph Jackson of the Jackson 5. Rather, he gave them appropriate love all the time – of both the soft and tough varieties. Within the band Dappy also played a role as motivator – encouraging Fazer to pull his weight, for instance.

B's striking down of their doubts was just one of many gifts diligently offered over the years. For instance, the way he assembled the equipment for the band in the studio was imaginative as well as generous. The speakers he gave to Fazer were a Christmas present, the keyboard was an abandoned instrument he had lying around in his house. Then he would get an unwanted microphone from somewhere and a computer somehow too, and before Tulisa and her band-mates knew it they had an impressively equipped functioning studio. Plato helped teach them how to use all the gear. However, it was B who truly moulded what became the N-Dubz style and attitude. As Fazer wrote, 'The main part of...the N-Dubz philosophy comes from him, no two ways about it.' It was almost as if B was the screenwriter of their story, guiding and shaping the themes of what would become the N-Dubz drama.

He was, in fact, a man of many roles and talents. Indeed, Fazer considered his uncle to be 'almost like a community leader' in the role he had in Tulisa's band. He wanted to get as many young people as possible out of the grips of temptation and negativity. He encouraged Tulisa, Fazer and Dappy to bring any of their friends to the studio so they could share in the fun and opportunities he wanted to provide. 'Bring all the ghetto boys here, bring them in here off the streets, man,' he would tell them. As the band remembered, he was never one to be intimidated. Sometimes the studio would be full of 'ghetto boys' and all manner of colourful characters. B would not be scared by this. Instead, he would walk in and act like he owned the place – which he did. In doing so, he won the respect of such folk, as they are rarely impressed by anyone in whom they sense fear. Mel, Tulisa's stepmother, has a more cynical theory regarding B and Plato's motivation. 'All that stuff about making them perform music to get them off the streets, I don't think that's the only reason,' she said. 'Byron and Plato also saw it as a way to make money.'

Make no mistake about it – B wanted to turn these people away from crime and negative, destructive behaviour. He wanted to keep Tulisa and her band-mates far away from such conduct, too. As Dappy candidly put it: 'He knew if he didn't help me I could get in trouble and maybe go to jail, or get hurt.' He even arranged for them to participate in a tour for the UK Crimestoppers charity. It was a strange choice for a band aiming at an urban market to take. Although Crimestoppers is an independent organisation it is perceived as being a wing of the police. As Fazer put it, the three band members 'hated the police' at this stage. However, B knew what he was doing. Firstly, he was subtly showing them that he did not want them pursuing a life of crime. Secondly, he was showing them that there were immediate rewards to be had by 'staying straight'. The reward was not just the live experience. They also earned £200 per night. Tulisa felt great: she was earning money for making music. Her sense of self-worth rose again. While the occasions of N-Dubz live performances sometimes seemed incongruous, bands cannot afford to be picky in their nascent times. Even pop royalty such as Take That and leading boy band The Wanted did scores of dates to tiny audiences of schoolchildren as they bid to make it in pop. Indeed, Take That even did a tour in conjunction with the Family Planning Association during their early days. It is fair to say that the finer points of contraception were not at the forefront of many of their fans' imaginations as they screamed at the hip-gyrating boys.

Sometimes the band would not take on a suggestion B made. For instance, he once said when they were discussing a promotional video that it should feature guitarists dressed in ninja suits. He then suggested that he and his brother would appear in the video. The band laughed off his suggestion and said there was no way they were letting them appear in one of their videos. In reply B told them: 'You're nothing, man, you're amateur to us, you little rascals! Shut up, Dappy, you're my sperm – you be quiet!' These moments of banter could not mask what was a mutually respectful relationship between the band and their mentor.

****

Romantic adventures continued and Tulisa's spiritual side also developed. The more sensible relationship she had embarked on in the wake of her tumultuous times was bearing fruit. Her partner had, in her words, been 'a player' prior to them getting together. At the start of their relationship they were quite laidback about things but they began to get slowly more serious about one another. Tulisa puts part of this down to her developing a belief and faith in God. Her religious awakening not only took her away from 'dark times' it also gave her a renewed sense of personal worth and esteem. Her partner reacted to this not by panicking as some men would but by feeling even more attracted to her. He did, she said, 'pack in the crap' and get serious with her at last.

Things got even more serious when they got drunk one night and decided to get engaged. It was, as Tulisa tells the story, more a mutual decision rather than a case of one or other of them getting down on bended knee. Indeed, the engagement was a 'facade' according to Tulisa. Nevertheless, as a 19-year-old and into her early twenties, she was engaged to be married. The relationship then ended. It had been more a matter of convenience for some time, with neither party willing at first to bring it to an official end. 'We were just in the groove and it was an easy thing to do,' she reflected later. Eventually they did split but Tulisa is keen to emphasise that this was not caused by any misbehaviour on her part. Rumours that they split after she had cheated on him are without foundation, she has said. She insists that as someone who is not oriented on sex she is always happy with just one man in her life. However, the fact remained that after she and her fiancé broke it off she was 21 and single. She had come a long way from those tumultuous times she endured after her painful break-up. By now she felt she was a 'fully empowered woman'. She was wiser and more confident partly as a result of the harsh experiences she had endured and partly as a result of her growing faith. The passage of time and the maturity that naturally grows as a result also had a part to play in the new Tulisa.

The next man in her life was actually a blast from her past – an 'old crush' of hers called Justin, whose stage name was Ultra. She had dated him before but nothing serious or lasting had come of it. This time they got on better. The communication was more honest and profound; a connection was made. Previously there had been some game-playing but as they became reacquainted, Tulisa felt the difference. As they embarked on a fresh, more serious relationship Tulisa spoke very positively of what they had together. She wrote in *Against All Odds*:

'Finally, this feels right. For the first time ever it feels like a completely comfortable and trusting relationship that's equal on both sides. It's my first time of being in love as a love should be.' Most significantly, she said she had finally become involved in a relationship because she *wanted* to be with someone rather than feeling she needed to be. She had, she felt, grown from a slightly needy girl into a woman who did not need or even want 'imitations of love'. Although her relationship with Justin was not to last, the confidence it ignited in her make it a highly significant milestone in her life. She felt and knew she deserved real love. It had just become a lot harder for any man to treat Tulisa badly, or for her to take herself into difficult, painful situations.

With her band gathering experience and momentum and her personal confidence the highest it had ever been, Tulisa could afford to feel optimistic that good times were ahead for her. How right she was. With their sound and image coming together, Tulisa's band wanted to push things to a new level. They wanted to be noticed. The band was beginning to gather some mentions in small journals. Meanwhile, they were building their own mini-library of photographs of themselves rehearsing, recording and performing live. They were ready to be introduced to the media. B assembled these together to build a home-made 'press kit' for the band. Were they signed to a record label the press relations team would have thrown its resources into compiling a kit of information and photographs with which to promote the act to the media. For Tulisa and her band-mates they had to start one step away. Their roughly assembled kit was put together to attract both a record label and the press. Anyone, in fact, who could or would help them up the musical ladder.

Assembling these kits and then posting them out was a mundane task for B. A painful one, too: he got paper cuts and even broke fingernails as he sent out many hundreds of missives on behalf of the band over a period of several months. The band members would then have to endure the three responses familiar to all who have tried to break into the music industry: mass silence, cold 'no thank you's and insincere interest. It was the third one that really got them down. They were so keen to get a record label or press attention that when people promised them the earth it was a painful blow to realise that the promises were not going to be kept.

These testing times were actually a useful education for Tulisa. The entertainment industry has plenty of fickle characters who will pay you lavish attention one moment and then disappear completely when they spot a more tempting or important person over your shoulder. This happens literally, at show business and music industry parties, and more metaphorically, where the flavour of the month is suddenly ruthlessly dropped as a new exciting prospect appears. Record companies lose interest overnight in backing a previously favoured act. The press builds up entertainers and other celebrities, casting them as the golden child of the day, only to either forget about them abruptly, or continue to write about them but in the most destructive, intrusive and negative of ways. Therefore, the insincere promises that she and her band received from B's mail-outs were useful lessons for them.

That said, the frustration soon became too much to bear for the man at the heart of guiding Tulisa's band. 'I'm not doing this package shit no more,' said B. However, rather than give up on the dream, he and the band all agreed that they had to change tack. There must be a better way to make it happen. They decided that a video of them was required in order to grab the attention of the industry. It was a wise choice. A video is always harder to ignore. Also, given the energy, cheek and attitude that were the strong point of the band, a moving image was always going to show them in their best light. For sultry acts that were low on charisma, a moody black-and-white still was the order of the day. For this band, the more energy the better.

The first steps for the band came when they recorded a song called 'Bad Man Riddim'. Their second single, 'Life is Getting Sicker By The Day', saw them garner more attention, thanks to the nationwide play it received on pirate radio. They changed their name in time to NW1, the postcode of Camden Town. They then recorded further demos, including tracks called 'Every Day Of My Life, 'Don't Feel Like Moving', 'Girl On Road' and 'Livin Broke'. Then they released a download-only single called 'You Better Not Waste My Time'. An early champion of their music was urban digital channel Channel U. Having originally got their rough promotional videos on to the channel's night time playlist they then broke onto the daytime playlist. Viewers were able to vote to see the video and they began to do so in numbers. The band noticed at their live shows that a lot of the audience seemed to be Channel U aficionados. People would also sometimes approach them in the street to ask if they were 'that band from Channel U'.

This was all a great boost to their spirits. Meanwhile, their energy continued to be boosted by B. Tulisa's insights into his workings are particularly moving. In the book *Against All Odds* she paints him as a man full of energy, ideas and love. Sometimes that love was tough, as we have already seen. For instance, when she arrived at the studio one day in a bad frame of mind due to her mother's ongoing health issues, he asked her why she was bringing to the studio with her 'all that shit at home that's doing your nut in' and, in doing so, doing the nuts in of her band-mates. At the time she was enraged by his words but when she looked back she saw how they were just what she and her band-mates needed.

However, there was a specific need in her over and above the band, and it was typical of B's loving, attentive nature that he noticed it. Following an unproductive day in the studio during which she had been enormously down, he drove her home. During that journey he gave her some advice that was prescient. He told her that a fact of life was that some people were 'depressives'. He told her, 'You need to accept that you are a depressed person. Don't try and fight it. Accept it, deal with it, live with it and get on with it.' He added that she should, in fact, go further and 'embrace' her depression. More than anything, her told her, she should never let her depression hold her back in life. This was useful advice, as Tulisa was facing some very dark times. 'I would always know when my mum was about to have an episode,' she told the *Daily Mail* later. 'She'd make dinner and the meat would be raw. She'd be lethargic one minute and then cleaning around the house unable to stop the next. I'd phone the hospital, explain her symptoms and they wouldn't want to know. I was young and they didn't take me seriously even though I was my mum's carer.

'In the end I'd have to take her to A&E to try to get her admitted. But often by the time I got back home from school the next day, the doctors would say they'd done an evaluation of her and she was fine to go home. Sometimes I would spend weeks taking her back and forward to A&E and then finally they would admit her and she'd be in hospital for up to three months….I started losing respect for my mum. She couldn't take care of herself so I didn't see how she thought she could take care of me. If I wanted to go out with my friends, I did it because I felt I had no one to answer to. But she'd leave me 60 voice messages on my mobile, send up to 30 texts a day, phone all our family and even the police to tell them I'd gone missing or was misbehaving. She didn't want my friends in the house and didn't want me to go out.'

Thank goodness for the salvation that music – and the band – gave her. As they faced the disappointments, let-downs and frustrations of their early years, B was creative and imaginative in his tips. Tulisa wrote that he sometimes lied in order to cheer them up, saying he would sometimes tell them things that were 'complete bollocks' just to raise their mood. 'It worked!' she added. However, they had fallings-out, too. During the last months of his life they had more or less stopped talking at one point. That stand-off ended when he phoned her up and told her that he wanted them to put the music to one side for a second as he wanted to remind her he was her uncle, regardless of their creative ventures. He told her that 'before all this you were just my little niece and I want that back'. He reminded her that he loved her. It is haunting to reflect that this was the last conversation they had.

CHAPTER
FOUR

Imagine poor Tulisa's torment when B died. Just two days earlier the band had played perhaps their most exciting show to date. 'I Swear' had been released and was receiving much airplay on Kiss FM. The audience was absolutely pumped for their arrival, greeting the band with screams. 'It was difficult to take in,' wrote Fazer later. The crowd got so manic that some of its members at the front actually pulled Fazer off the stage and into the audience. Dappy leapt in to retrieve his band-mate. Fazer looked over and saw B watching from the wings. The look of joy and pride in their mentor's face was clear. Fazer would later recall the evening as one of the best moments of his life. The following day, he met up with B to discuss which studio the band might move to as the contract for their current studio was nearing its end. It was the last time a member of N-Dubz would see its founder alive. The day after, Fazer and Dappy had to break into B's house after becoming concerned about his disappearance, when he had failed to collect Dappy's mother from the airport as planned. It was Fazer who discovered B's body. He had died sitting in front of the television, with the set tuned in to Channel U. It transpired he had died from a heart attack. Tulisa meanwhile was elsewhere, unaware of the tragedy.

B had almost predicted the day was imminent. He would sometimes say to the band, 'One day you guys will be here on your own and I won't be here to look after you,' or remind them 'I won't be here forever.' As with so much of what B had told the group, these predictions turned out to be true. He had seemed ill in the time leading up to his passing. He kept coughing, remembered Fazer, and also vomited a few times. The signs, it was only clear in retrospect, had been there for some time. Dappy was naturally devastated when he realised his father had died. At first he did not want to enter the room Fazer had discovered the body in. After a while he walked in and helped lay B's body on the sofa. He covered the body with a blanket and then left the room, absolutely gutted. The next thing that he and Fazer had to do was decide how to break the news to Tulisa, who was busy filming *Dubplate Drama* at the time. It was not to be an easy moment.

Ironically, she was filming a scene in which her character had burst into tears after learning someone she loved had died. She cut an onion up when she had to cry during a scene. When merely cutting the onion didn't do the trick, she simply held the two halves of the onion directly against

50

her eyes. The production team also used a tear stick to help spark the sobs. Art was mirroring life in the most painful way. Tulisa had found that the best way to prepare for such a scene was to imagine that she really had been bereaved in real life. Just before she filmed the scene she had been sitting imagining how she would feel if she lost someone dear to her. Meanwhile, Fazer and Dappy were discussing how best to tell her that her beloved Uncle B had died. That same day, she turned her mobile phone on to discover a rash of texts from her two band-mates. All the messages said were that they needed to speak to her soon about something important.

She immediately feared the worst and phoned Dappy to ask what the matter was. He would not tell Tulisa over the phone and instead arranged to drive to the filming location to tell her in person. Meanwhile, the cast and crew members did their best to comfort Tulisa as her mind raced through a series of tragic possibilities. A feeling inside her grew. She tried to phone other family members as she waited in the hope that they could tell her what had happened. As fate would have it she could not get through to anyone by phone. When Dappy and Fazer arrived, Tulisa could not wait for them to get to the heart of the matter and tell her what was going on. She quickly lost her patience and shouted at them, demanding they just come out and tell her. Dappy told her to sit down and prepare for some bad news. He then said: 'Are you ready for this? B's dead.' Tulisa's body went immediately into shock. She felt her heart rate soar as the news sunk in. Her last memory was a fear that she was going to have a heart attack. Then she remembers falling and someone holding her as she sank to the ground. She eventually came to and became hysterical. She cried floods of tears and made the sort of loud wailing noise that is only ever made by someone in the immediate stages of grief.

'I couldn't stop it,' she recalled in *Against All Odds*. 'They took me out on to a patch of grass outside and I kept crying hysterically.' After a while she composed herself and faced the obvious reality that while she had lost an uncle and a mentor, her band-mate Dappy had lost something even more intensely precious – a father. So she hugged him and offered her condolences. At the time, she remembered later, Dappy was absolutely cold with grief. There was no crying or outward signs of grieving; instead he was 'numb', she said. They got a lift home and sat in silence in the back seat of the car. It was a beautiful spring evening and they were sitting in the back of a convertible car with the roof down. What should have been an almost idyllic experience was instead laced with tragedy. They held hands and dealt silently with their emotions.

The following day the band was booked to perform a live show. Initially, they felt they were unable to fulfil the booking. However, with Fazer taking the lead in this, the band decided that they would honour the commitment. B had worked so hard to get them where they were. Surely pressing on with their career was the only way to honour him. Indeed, as Fazer reminded Tulisa and Dappy, B had seemingly died while waiting to see the band's video on television. When they took to the stage their emotions were raw. His supportive presence from the wings was a stark omission. At the end of the show they were pleased to have honoured not just the booking, but the memory of their father and uncle. Then the sense of grief came flooding over them once more.

For Tulisa, grief was not the only challenging emotion. She almost felt a sense of responsibility, bordering on guilt. Even though the two had settled their differences before he died, she still felt that the pressures of working for the band had made him ill, and ultimately claimed his life. She wrote in *Against All Odds*: 'All the stress and pressure that came from getting us to where we were pretty much killed him, so he died for our success.' Strong words and a sentiment echoed by Fazer in the song 'Papa', where he sings: 'It's like you sacrificed your life, for the love of success and a life full of stress.' He repeated the sentiment in the same book as Tulisa. Dappy was hardest hit, of course. He too felt that B's death had been caused in part by his efforts on their behalf. 'Obviously, we never had much money and he spent it all and got unhealthy, just smoking and the stress of thinking, "Am I going to get them to the top?"' said Dappy. He was left feeling very alone in the world. 'He guided me for 18 years,' he said a few years later. 'He was my dad and my best friend, that's why I called him B, never Dad. When he died I was lost.' All three band members continue to this day to be guided and motivated in their lives by their memories of their hero.

The band needed to face these horrific emotions

together. The loss of B made them closer and tighter as people and as a band. Remarkably, even in death, B was firing them onwards and fuelling their energy and ambition. An early watershed moment in the post-B era came when they won a MOBO award. It was in the Best UK Newcomer category, which had been voted for by viewers of the ITV local news programme *London Tonight*. They were up against Tinchy Stryder, Mutya Buena, Sadie Ama and UnkleJam. Tulisa had been convinced that the award would go to Mutya Buena rather than her act. There was a huge cheer when N-Dubz was announced as the winner. Tulisa strode to the stage alongside Dappy and Fazer. Dappy took the award and led the audience in a chant of 'Naa Naa Niiii'. After thanking members of the band's management, his mother and friends, Dappy said: 'Most of all I want to say thank you to my Dad, rest in peace. RIP, thank you very much.' He then passed the microphone to Tulisa who thanked the fans, her family and 'most of all Uncle B for putting his heart and soul into us and getting us where we are today.' Securing the award had been so important for the band – all the more so because of B's death. Tulisa felt that Dappy in particular 'couldn't bear the thought of not getting it' after all they had been through. Elsewhere that evening, Amy Winehouse was crowned best female vocalist while Dizzee Rascal was named best male. However, for N-Dubz the evening was all about honouring Uncle B. Tulisa said later that they felt his spirit was present in the arena. The band would go on to win further MOBO awards.

In the months that followed, Tulisa looked back over the influence that B had on her life, both musically and beyond. Memories kept flashing back, including the time he taught her karate during a family holiday in Greece. He had not merely shown her the physical moves but also the more esoteric and emotional techniques behind them, including the concepts of 'cleansing the soul, positive and negative energy and that kind of thing'. She said that many of his concepts about spirituality helped influence her own spiritual and ultimately religious journey (a journey we shall return to in due course).

What a legacy he had left in the life of his treasured niece. He would have been delighted to see that in the wake of his death, all his devoted hard work began to pay off. Finally, the band was going places. In 2007 they signed to Polydor Records. To get a record deal with such a label was a major success for them. The UK arm of the label has released the material of hit acts including Slade, Girls Aloud, Kaiser Chiefs, The Saturday and S Club 7. Internationally it has released the work of the likes of the Black Eyed Peas – a band N-Dubz have sometimes been compared with – Emimen, Queens of the Stone Age and Pussycat Dolls. What a prestigious rostrum Tulisa, Dappy and Fazer were joining. Their first release on Polydor was a reissue of 'You Better Not Waste My Time'. It reached UK No 26. The band considered this 'a result', particularly given that it had been released previously.

Then, in 2008, the band released a new song called 'Ouch'. The video for the song was uploaded to YouTube and received four million views within a month. It was clear that Tulisa's music was connecting with the public. However, the relationship between the band and their label soured soon after when the band played Polydor some of their other songs. The label bigwigs were not having any of it. They disliked everything they heard, including 'Ouch' and 'Papa'. Having rejected many of the band's songs – which felt like precious babies to Tulisa, Fazer and Dappy – Polydor then made broader efforts to mould the band into a different outfit. First, the label suggested that song-writers join the band in composing new songs. The band felt that the aim of this was to take them in a different direction – not a direction they were happy to go in. They gave Polydor's ideas a go, including a studio session with a producer and songwriter who had worked with George Michael and *X Factor* winner Leona Lewis, respectively. 'It wasn't us,' reflected Tulisa, who felt they would have been selling out to go along with Polydor's plans.

She actually felt that Polydor simply did not understand what N-Dubz were about. This is a far from uncommon complaint from bands signed to big labels. Often, the reality is that the label actually *does* understand what a band is about, but simply wants the band to be about something different. She also complained that Polydor had insufficient faith in them. None of the label's doubts did anything to shake her belief in what N-Dubz could achieve. She thought Polydor were nothing short of 'completely mad' for not supporting them and their vision. Her suspicion was that Polydor wanted to make them appeal to a broader age group than the band had in mind. In fairness, it would have been a stretch to make a band true to the original N-Dubz vision appeal to any substantial numbers of music fans above the age of 30. The end was nigh, and the band say it was a symbolic moment that made them decide to ditch Polydor. They were travelling to a gig and their van pulled into a petrol station. Tulisa, Dappy and Fazer hopped out and were recognised by a young girl. She told them she remembered them: 'You had that song out ages ago.' Whether this is one of those 'legends' that get written into a band's history, or an entirely authentic story, it certainly crystallises the fears that Tulisa had at the time. Two immediate and undesirable options existed: toeing the Polydor line and watering down their vision, or giving up entirely and becoming one of music's could-have-been stories, not even memorable enough to exist in a 'whatever happened to' pub discussion.

Instead, they eyed a musical 'third way': audaciously cutting their ties with Polydor and seeking a new label to call home. Many established acts leave a big record label but to do so at such a fledgling point in one's career takes particular self-confidence. Tulisa had rarely lacked belief in the band, neither had Dappy and Fazer. Their self-assurance had been given a major boost by the arrival of their new legendary manager, Professor Jonathan Shalit. He was best known for having discovered Welsh singer Charlotte Church, who sold more than 5 million CDs with him, and for his 'rediscovery' of harmonica player Larry Adler, who recorded an album with him featuring the likes of Cher, Sir

Elton John and Sting. He has also guided and managed the careers of Myleene Klass, Lorraine Kelly and Kelly Brook. He has also been a successful manager of urban-styled acts, including Jamelia and Big Brovaz, who both enjoyed critical and commercial success while under his wing and won eight MOBO awards between them. He is a regular in industry power lists and has himself estimated dining at the Ivy restaurant hundreds of times a year. The owner even once even took out an advertisement in an industry magazine thanking Shalit for his regular custom! Shalit has been described as 'a legend in his own lunchtime'.

Shalit had expressed an interest in managing the band even before B passed away. Tulisa said that while her uncle had initially been opposed to the idea he had begun to change his mind a few days before his death. They were left in need of a new mentor and when they researched Shalit's track record they were, naturally, very impressed. They met him and decided to sign up with his company, Roar Global. It is a relationship that continues to this day. After leaving Polydor they signed to a smaller label called All Around The World. The label's announcement of its new acquisition included a howler of a mistake. It read: 'MOBO award-winning N-Dubz have found a new home with AATW. Hailing from Camden in south London the trio's music has variably been described as hip-hop, garage and RnB but their style is pretty unique, blending traditional song structure and inspired lyrics with distinctly urban elements and influences.' The description of their musical sound was close enough to the mark, but given how central Camden Town has always been to the band's image, it was a particularly bad error for the label to describe Camden, arguably the most celebrated district of north London, as being in south London.

The band added its own statement to the announcement. It was a diverting combination of confidence and cheek. 'You've heard of us, even if you don't know it yet,' it began. 'Remember that boy driving you mad every morning on the No 42? The one playing music on his mobile at full volume? He's listening to our music. So is his sister, his best mate, his best mate's older brother and his teacher. Throughout our career we've strived to become masters of the melody, kings of the chorus and rulers of the ad lib, simply put we balance straight-up pop smashes with a street smart style and our music's for everyone. We make songs for your mum, your dad and your nan.' After adding some more background to their act, and also revealing some of their signature sayings, it concluded with an ebullient promise. 'We know it's rare to come across a group you totally believe in and there are a lot of good acts in the UK, but great ones? Not so many, but we definitely aim to change that...'

They would succeed in their aim but first there was to be more trouble and controversy. By this stage, Tulisa needed to respond to something that she would become quite familiar with in the years to come: controversy erupting around her cousin Dappy. He recorded a song called 'Love For My Slum' with another artist, and then filmed a promotional video for it. In one 10-second segment of the video, Dappy stands next to a character labelled as 'rich boy' and angrily warns, then punches the rich boy, who falls to the ground. A newspaper asked whether the video encouraged young music fans to pursue a life of 'criminality', adding that 'senior members' of the Metropolitan police believed it certainly did. Superintendent Leroy Logan of Hackney police, a former Chairman of the Black Police Association, spoke of 'Those out there who are keen on hijacking the [grime music] scene, and using these videos to spread negativity, anger, and aggression. And whether the messages are coded or explicit, they often play themselves out on the street.'

Another extra-curricular venture Dappy took part in was a track called 'Babylon Fi Get Shot', which he recorded alongside another rapper called Face Killa. For those unfamiliar with street lingo, the song's title translates roughly as 'Police to get shot'. He has since distanced himself from the song and the sentiment. 'I was young and dumb, and I've grown up a lot since then. I'm an adult now and turned my back on those views a long time ago as they are wrong,' he said. 'Doing the job I do now has made me realise you don't have to hate the police and be negative about them. N-Dubz are all about positivity.'

However, he also made more positive appearances in the mainstream media, which in turn brought Tulisa further into the public mind. In the autumn of 2007, he appeared on the BBC's music panel show *Never Mind The Buzzcocks*. Host Simon Amstell described him as being part of 'urban collective N-Dubz'. He soon made jokes at

Dappy's expense, saying that Lee Ryan from the boy band Blue had been booked but had pulled out at the last moment, adding: 'I won't say who replaced him, I shouldn't say that, should I, N-Dubz?'

Dappy then produced one of his famous hats, and asked the audience: 'Who wants to see Simon wear a Dappy hat?'

He threw the hat to Amstell who calmly placed it to one side, and carried on with the show, promising 'I'll wear it later.' In due course, he encouraged Dappy to remove his own hat so the audience could see how he looked without it. As Dappy obliged, Amstell commented: 'It's Kenzie from Blazin' Squad.'

Noel Fielding said: 'I was thinking more Stan Laurel.' He added that the hat made him look like a 'woollen dog' or a 'knitted poodle'. Dappy might have preferred to be a Doberman, if he had to be a dog at all. He took it all in as good humour as he could, though. Tulisa, too, must have giggled when she watched it.

There was plenty more fun surrounding Dappy during the show. He tried – and failed – to lead the audience in a sing-along of George Michael's 'Careless Whisper'. It's always cringe-worthy when such attempts fall flat. He then joked that Willie Nelson looked 'perverse' in a video they were shown. He then joked that it looked as if Nelson was saying to a woman with his smile, 'If I had you alone for two seconds I would smash your back doors in.' He said that Camden Town is the capital of London, asking the audience, 'Who knows about Camden Town?' only to be met by silent indifference.

'Please stop talking to them,' pleaded Amstell.

Dappy threatened Fielding, saying that 'the people who listen to my music' would take him to task for mocking his hat. He and Phil Jupitus made hard work of the 'intros' round in which they perform the introduction of a song for the third team member to guess. Why, Amstell asked Dappy, did he give him a hat with a smaller bobble than his? 'That was the last one I had under my bed,' replied Dappy. All in all, it had been a memorable appearance by Dappy, whose quirky charisma had captured the attention of viewers and consequently brought N-Dubz to the attention of new people. He would go on to become quite the *Buzzcocks* cult legend.

Tulisa, too, was appearing on television in 2007 and was pleased to have a foot in an industry in which she had long held aspirations to work. As we have seen, she appeared in the UK television series *Dubplate Drama*. When it was launched in the autumn of 2005, *Dubplate Drama* caught the attention of viewers as it was billed as the world's first interactive drama series. It followed characters including MC Shystie and a female MC called Dionne. Tulisa, who was 17 when it launched, loved watching it, describing it as 'the best thing I had ever seen'. She felt that here was a programme that was 'pretty much' about her and her friends. Viewers would be given the chance to vote on the outcome of each episode, an exciting melding of the drama and the popular reality television formats of the likes of *Big Brother* and the *X Factor* with their public votes. 'We made it interactive because we want young people to talk about the various issues raised by the weekly dilemmas,' said co-founder Michelle Clothier, of the youth marketing group Livity. 'Young people have less loyalty to brands and programmes than before so we wanted to use as many media as possible.'

Tulisa loved *Dubplate Drama* so much that she would sit and daydream about getting to appear in it one day. She was hooked for the entire first series and could not have been more excited when the programme makers approached her to be a part of the second series. Originally, she was considered to take the role of – in her words – a 'slutty chick', but in the end Tulisa took a more serious and emotional part, in the shape of a character called Laurissa. From playing Tallulah in *Bugsy Malone* and now Laurissa in *Dubplate Drama*, it seemed that Tulisa was attracting parts whose names corresponded to parts of her own name. For the next series she got an even bigger part, as she had impressed the production team first time around. Her *Dubplate* character was a cocaine addict who was in pop group The Fam and got abused by her manager and boyfriend 'Prangers', played by Ricci Harnett. It was not to be a light-hearted experience. That said, she performed the part well and would return to the show for subsequent seasons, as would Dappy.

However, their main focus remained musical. They wanted to do justice to legacy of Uncle B by producing a winning debut album. To make plain that the effort was to be a tribute to him, they dropped the original title and named it after him.

Coventry Central Library

Tel 024 7683 2314
Fax 024 7622 0465

Borrowed Items 21/02/2018 16 08
XXXXXXXXX5540

Item Title	Due Date
* Tulisa	21/03/2018
* Wherever you are	21/03/2018

* Indicates items borrowed today

Thank you for using this unit - Cenself03

coventry.gov.uk/libraries
central.library@coventry.gov.uk
Monday, Tuesday, Wednesday, Thursday,
Friday 9.00am - 7.00pm
Saturday 9.00am - 4.30pm
Sunday 12.00-4.00pm
Sunday 12.00noon - 4.00pm

CHAPTER
FIVE

The upward trajectory in the career of Tulisa, Dappy and Fazer was crystallised when their first album was released in November 2008. They had originally planned to name it *Against All Odds*, but actually called it *Uncle B*, in honour of the man who had been pivotal in the band's early days. Rarely in the modern era are debut albums so long in coming – the band themselves estimate that *Uncle B* was made over a period of eight years. As Fazer noted, it was almost like a 'best of' effort, as every song on the album had already been released via one route or another prior to the album's release. It entered the UK charts in a high position: No 11. In Ireland it fared less well, only reaching No 36. The first full track on the album is 'Wouldn't You', and opens – after a brief and tame 'Na Na Nii' from Dappy – with Tulisa's soulful lyrics. Nonetheless it is quite a low-key song with which to open an album effectively. Certainly compared to some of the stompers that would appear on future N-Dubz albums this is a tame affair. Within a few lines of 'Strong Again', the ante has been upped as Dappy confesses to violence. The music is fiercer as he bemoans getting community service as a result of his misdeeds. Tulisa takes over in the chorus, and then handles the next verse. Opening a theme that would become a regular concern for the band, Tulisa reminds listeners that life is short. A similar sentiment appears in 'Don't Get Nine'.

'I Swear' blends Tulisa's singing and Dappy's intense raps with an upbeat hip-hop/grime track. She mourns having lied and delivers a convincing tone of regret. The lie had involved cheating by the girl in the song. Typically for the land of N-Dubz, she is caught out after her man spots an unknown pair of Nike trainers and then seeing her kissing another man. In 'Ouch', the issue of infidelity is tackled again but this time it is the man cheating. Tulisa's high vocals are impressive. The backing track includes piano and violin. 'It's all about a whole debate between a woman and man after finding out the man's cheated,' she said. 'It's just a whole storyline, the whole aftermath of it. The video's got a whole storyline too that people can relate to.' There are also strings at the start of 'Love For My Slum'. Other notable tracks on the album include 'Feva Las Vegas'. Tulisa complains in it that success can provoke jealousy, even among friends. Was this a reflection of issues she had faced? In 'Sex', Dappy spares no blushes or details. Then comes 'Secrets', a tamer affair set to an acoustic guitar. 'Dappy, turn my mike up,' requests Tulisa before revealing that in the song she is going to reveal a thing or two about herself. Dappy then joins the vocals to reassure her that she is not alone.

'Papa Can You Hear Me' is, of course, the band's tribute to Uncle B. Very emotional it is, too. David Balls was – as he acknowledged – rather harsh in his assessment of the song on the website Digital Spy. 'The mix of uber-serious rapping and abrasive beats is fundamentally awkward, while their lyrics are as crass as they are heartfelt. By showing their softer side, the Camden collective are probably hoping to win some new fans, but they should probably stick to making hip-hop bangers in the futureside,' he wrote. It is hard to agree: this song quickly became and remains a central part of the N-Dubz musical canon. Dappy's tribute to his late father might not be as gentle as some musical tributes are but in its own, rough-around-the-edges way, it is a tearjerker and a heartstring puller. The album closes with 'Outro'.

Due in part to the somewhat obscure label it was released by, and the fact it was a debut, the album was not reviewed widely in the mainstream media. Describing the album as being made by 'the sort of young people who wake *Daily Mail* readers up in a sweat,' a reviewer on the *In The News* website described Tulisa as the band's 'chief warbler' and complimented her on her 'impressive chest'. He concluded that the band should not be dismissed and compared them to punk legends the Sex Pistols. He said his readers should 'Buy this album and enjoy it for what it is:

the sound of young Britain. Resistance is futile.' Tulisa will have found it hard not to smile at the compliment paid to her chest. Another review brought to her attention was that on the Orange website. It concluded: 'Parents won't be too impressed, mind you, but *Uncle B* will likely be lauded for its furious party jams made with the *Skins* generation of reckless teens in mind. All that, and it's actually quite a good listen.' The RapReviews.com website said: 'All in all, N-Dubz have coughed up an impressive debut that has been a long time coming.' The reviewer, Jesal 'Jay Soul' Padania, identified Tulisa's place in the band thus: 'You have two rappers, one of whom sings a lot, and a single white female taking care of choruses and a few verses.'

Unfortunately, one of the more mainstream outlets to review the album was less impressed. The *Observer*'s Sam Wolfson gave the album three out of five stars, but the actual main body of his review was more damning than that score implied. Indeed, the only thing he could find to praise it for was what he saw as its unintentional humour. 'N-Dubz are like So Solid Juniors – three youngsters with lyrics so tame they've been allowed to play UK secondary schools,' he wrote. In conclusion, he referred to a character from the BBC sketch-show comedy *Little Britain*: 'N-Dubz's inadvertent satire of adolescent attitudes is far more astute than Vicky Pollard's. Shame they take themselves so seriously.' In the *Guardian*, Alex Macpherson praised the work ethic and 'raw talent' of N-Dubz and its manifestation in their debut album. He wrote that Tulisa 'attempts to intervene with keening vocals' on N-Dubz Vs

NAA, and noted that she and Dappy trade 'rat-a-tat back-and-forth barbs' on 'Don't Get Nine'. He enjoyed both, saying they 'seem more like stage productions than tracks, and are much more compelling than some of the more standard cuts.'

The album sold well enough to reach platinum status within three months of its release, and ultimately sold over 500,000 copies. The band was guardedly pleased with their progress. They had gone with their instincts in signing up with the new label and manager. A key part of the appeal for both was the degree of creative control the band was being offered. Dappy and Fazer considered themselves the 'A&Rs' – the acronym given to the 'artists and repertoire' staff who act as a liaison between the label and artist. 'We chose the records that are gonna come out and decide on how we are gonna sound, no one else – it's our ting dis,' claimed Dappy, seemingly writing Tulisa out of the decision-making process. However, Fazer made clear that if Tulisa did not approve of an idea they came up with then that idea would not go ahead. The lady herself was delighted with the success of *Uncle B* and reflected afresh that labels who had turned them away would be regretting that decision.

They embarked on a major tour to promote the album. In homage to the man as much as the album title they called it the Uncle B Tour. Originally it was to be a 16-date tour but such was the demand for tickets that the band added five extra shows. They played small-to-medium sized venues. For instance, in London they appeared at the Shepherds

Bush Empire and Indigo2. Each venue has a capacity of over 2,000 people. For Tulisa these were busy times. As the band had rehearsed for the tour she had been filming her part for the third series of *Dubplate Drama*. She had to condense the filming into one manic fortnight while simultaneously preparing for the upcoming gigs. The next single the band released was 'Strong Again'. A promotional video was filmed and everything seemed set for the song to be released. However, the physical release of the song on CD was cancelled But the download version of the single alone managed to get them to No 24 in the charts.

With the increased profile the album had given them, Tulisa and her band mates branched out. In 2009, she and N-Dubz contributed to a fundraising song for the charity War Child. It is a small but effective organisation that works hard on behalf of children whose families, communities and schools have been torn apart by war. They contributed to the song 'I Got Soul' – a reworked version of The Killers' 'All These Things That I've Done'. For the recording they put together a one-off band called Young Soul Rebels, which included Tinchy Stryder and Pixie Lott. 'We know lots of the acts taking part like Tinchy and Pixie, so it was a great vibe recording the song,' said Tulisa at the recording. For Tulisa this was a cause she had never previously thought about. As such, she felt pleased to have been given the chance to learn about it and make an effort at contributing to the support of such vulnerable children. Having been a child in need herself in a different scenario she has a special warmth for the plight of all kids who are hard done by. 'It's an issue that hasn't been looked at enough,' she said. 'And you know, even until I found out about this event, I didn't really know that much about it, and that's saying something you know,' she told BBC *Newsbeat*. 'And the fact that I'm only finding out now is not really good enough. So that was every reason for me to get involved.' The band then encountered a sense of how it feels to be No 1 when Tinchy Stryder's song of that name reached the top spot in April 2009. 'Wouldn't You' was released by N-Dubz as the final single to be lifted from *Uncle B*.

Another way that Tulisa spread her profile was by joining social networking websites. Acts such as Justin Bieber and Lily Allen have swelled their fame and fan base this way. Tulisa was to have a love/hate relationship with such online marketing. Later in her career she would build up a fearsome following on Twitter, but her first experiences with social networking were not happy ones. 'I'm not [on Facebook]... I was, but Facebook themselves deleted me, because they thought I was a fake version of myself,' she told the *Sunday Mirror*. She added that some of her Facebook interactions had been nothing short of farcical. 'There are about 60 fake Facebook pages of me. I've actually had arguments with myself on there,' she said. 'I'll message them saying, "Look, I know you're not me because I'm Tulisa". And they'll reply, "No, you're not, I'm Tulisa."'

One aspect of online presence that many celebrities have struggled with is the way that stories – often untrue – can take on a whole life of their own in the Wild West atmosphere that pervades the internet. In comparison to the way things can erupt over Twitter, the old-fashioned media can sometimes seem quaint and tame in comparison. When Tulisa made some light-hearted quips about how the infidelity of men might lead her to considering some same-sex relationships, she saw this trend in action. It all started with some observations about the often wayward behaviour of men after a man in her life had cheated on her. 'They all cheat, but most of them get away with it,' she said. 'I'm jealous because I know men. I think there are five per cent of men that stay faithful, but there's another 95 per cent out there that are absolute animals. Because I know that nearly all men cheat, it makes me hard to trust them and I would quite happily pay a bird to go and shag my man, record it, and if they gave me evidence I would pay them a grand.'

As online chatterers cast this joke as some sort of official coming-out moment, Tulisa looked with shock and amusement. 'People might think it's weird, but I was right, wasn't I? He was cheating.' She added: 'If I was going to get married, the first thing I'd do would be to send out a private detective. I've actually got the number for a cheating detective in my phone. When I get married, I will 100 per cent do a lie-detector test with him and ask if he's cheated. Why is it hardcore? If he hasn't cheated, it'll be fine. I've got a couple of issues, but it's not my fault I've been with f**ked-up men all my life.' She continued the denial later. 'I do hate men but I'm not gay. I'm not looking for a girlfriend,' she told *RWD* magazine. 'That tune was just fun and the video was spontaneous when I kissed NY. We were sat in the dressing room and I was trying to work out how to get her in the video. I was joking that we should have some 'lezza' action but I thought, "Let's make her the card dealer then at the end you'll find out she's my chick." You don't see on the video fully but we actually kissssssed.' That said, she has joked that she has considered hypnotherapy to make her a lesbian as she believes that women are so much more considerate as partners than men are. 'Women treat people so much better in a relationship,' she said. 'They don't have a d*ck to think for them.'

CHAPTER
SIX

In October 2009, Tulisa and Fazer sat in for BBC Radio1 Xtra presenter DJ Semtex. During the show, she performed a hilarious impersonation of the singer Chipmunk. 'This is turning into a mad two hours,' she said. (She can also convincingly impersonate an Australian accent and has had a crack at imitating her cousin Dappy.) They also spoke about and previewed the second N-Dubz album, *Against All Odds*. When *Uncle B* was released, one critic had – quite rightly – praised N-Dubz for the work rate they showed in putting together their debut album. Well, for their follow-up effort the band would work even harder. 'We've just taken a quick break,' Tulisa told the *Daily Star*, announcing that they had returned to the studio in earnest. 'We're having fun and the album is sounding good.' She added that they were keeping odd hours while working in the studio. 'We normally work till 5am – I come alive at midnight, like a vampire,' she said. As Fazer put it, they were in a hurry so they 'got our skates on' and often worked for up to 20 hours at a time. 'The work rate was crazy,' he said, accurately. The work paid off: their second album was completed in around four and a half months. It would be titled *Against All Odds* and was released in November 2009. (All three N-Dubz studio albums would be released in the month of November, and their 2011 *Greatest Hits* also hit the shelves that month.)

Tulisa wrote that they 'tried to be clever' during the composition of the songs for *Against All Odds*, by attempting to include contemporary references and also themes that their fans would relate to. It seemed a sensible, if obvious, approach to take. However, they also followed the maxim to write about what you know about. In songs such as 'Should Have Put Something On', their own concerns are clear. The song looks at becoming a parent at a young age, as experienced by Dappy. Given the lengthy gestation of their debut, the band was pleased to have the chance to put out an album that constituted a more immediate reflection of where they were. They aimed to make an album with sharp messages about the world and life for young people. Its short opener – that clocks in at just 57 seconds – forms a theme-setting intro to the album. It begins with a double chant of 'NaNaNiiii' and proceeds to set a bunker mentality. Again offering thanks and credit to Uncle B, it nonetheless insists that their success came, in the song's title, 'Against All Odds'. Next comes 'I Need You', a track accurately described as their 'biggest, most bombastic moment yet' by Digital Spy. Dappy noted that it was 'up-to-date and about Facebook and stuff'. It covers the experience of meeting a hot person in a club but losing touch with them after failing to take their phone number. The story is told from the point of view of both genders.

Then comes the comparatively mellower yet still fast-moving in the chorus 'Playing With Fire'. It is another narrative split between a male and female perspective. Here, the woman has discovered the man is cheating on her. However much she tries to get him to confess he won't back down. Its infectious call-and-response chorus is its most distinctive part. Live, that section has become fun, with Tulisa adding a 'Yes you bloody well did, mate' to the end. Indeed, the song casts Tulisa perfectly as the cheated-on but savvy and plucky girl who checks her man's texts and refuses to let him off the hook. (As one reviewer noted, had this been a real-life story one could only imagine what horrors she might find in Dappy's text inbox.)

The sequencing runs well into 'Say It's Over', a song about the difficulties of ending a relationship. Tulisa asks in the chorus how she can find the words to say the relationship is over. The pain and confusion in her voice is authentic and palpable. This is a lighter tune than its predecessors but it is no softie, and is livened-up by regular chanting from Dappy and Fazer in the background. The next song, which features Wiley, is called 'Na Na'. It is an unremarkable, high-energy rap tune that suffers in part from the low profile Tulisa takes. 'Shoulda Put Something On' features Dappy rapping harshly about his regrets at becoming a father so young in life. Tulisa sings the titular lyric soulfully in the background as Dappy vents his anger. She then sings of her rage at the man of the lyrics. Those who claim that N-Dubz is a terrible influence on the young would do well to consider how positive this message promoting safe sex is to the young. 'It's not something any of us have been through personally,' Tulisa told the *Daily Star* of the song's narrative. 'But everyone knows someone who has. The three of us wrote down our different perspectives and we based the song around that. It's our favourite track on the album.'

One of the album's other major message-based songs is 'No One Knows', which they wrote with Take That's Gary Barlow. It proved to be very timely, covering as it does the financial difficulties which were just beginning in the world and which have – to date – plagued it ever since. It preaches a message of unity in the face of the crisis. It also tells the young that everything they need is closer to them than it seems. Again, the band that has been widely vilified was preaching useful and positive messages to their impressionable and often generally disillusioned fan base. As Fazer commented, it was about fighting through the problems as a team.

The next song in the track listing is 'Number One'. It features Tinchy Stryder, and made history when released as a single – it was the first song called 'Number One' to reach that position in the UK singles chart. The song is about the fact that love is sometimes unfathomable. It is surprisingly touching for an N-Dubz effort. The BBC website commented that the song had 'Nice lyrics about feelings taking you over when you least expect them to. We've all been there, right?' So emotional is the song it could almost spark a tear from the listener. Is that the sound of N-Dubz going all sweet and sensitive on us? It sure is, and the sweetness is not over. In fact the next track is another sensitive affair – and features Tulisa alone on the vocals. In 'Comfortable', she wonders whether what she is feeling is love, or whether she is just comfortable. She worries that if they split she will lose her best friend in the world. It is a song of emotional intensity and one that showcases Tulisa's abilities well. In taking the vocals alone she opened a path for herself to consider a solo career.

For the remainder of the album sensitivity is in short supply, as we return to the sorts of themes more generally more associated with the band. 'Let Me Be' features Greek vocals, in a nod to the roots of two of the band members. Then Dappy concludes that the reason some women like him is that they have seen him on TV and assume he is richer than he is. Tulisa surfaces briefly to sing about needing space, in this somewhat low-key and muddled song. However, the song did reflect the band's mixed feelings about fame. They at once enjoy it and also wish that, from time to time, people could let them be. The album then ends with an outro of 'Against All Odds', which is essentially the same as the intro that opens the album. There had been plans to name their debut album *Against All Odds*, but this was changed after the death of Uncle B.

Could the band's underdog-titled album take them beyond such status to a more mainstream position? The sales were encouraging from the start. *Against All Odds* sold 300,000 in its first four weeks on sales. It had taken *Uncle B* five months to reach the same benchmark. They could also measure their progress in the media attention the album received. Where their debut had been ignored by the majority of the mainstream media's critics – and damned by many of those who did pen reviews of it – *Against All Odds* received far wider and more positive coverage. Well, it certainly divided the critics. A spectacularly negative review on the Irish show business website Entertainment.ie moaned: 'The problem is that their brand of music is such lowest-common-denominator stuff that it manages to offend even those that it's aimed at through its sheer awfulness.' The reviewer, Lauren Murphy, soon turned to Tulisa's song. 'Even the one Tulisa-led song – "Comfortable" – makes the mistake of using "dual carriageway", a phrase that not even Maria Callas herself could have made sound beautiful.'

Will Dean, in the *Guardian*, was more positive: 'While it's hardly exploding with originality, and the various references to Facebook and how many records they've sold do grate, this is a record brimming with vitality and chutzpah.' He gave the album three out of five stars.

The BBC website described *Against All Odds* as: 'An honest, authentic audio document of contemporary teenage Britain.' The reviewer Mike Diver showed he had captured a dimension of their music that had eluded some other critics when he concluded: 'All should be thankful it's almost exclusively positive of message – if you can dream it, you could well achieve it.' David Balls of *Digital Spy* also sang the album's praises, while dividing those who would or would not appreciate the new collection of songs. He wrote: 'Snottier listeners won't be convinced ... but many, many others will enjoy *Against All Odds*, a strong, cohesive collection that places N-Dubz at the forefront of British pop. A position, you suspect, they'll be taking up with relish.' Balls also singled out Tulisa's own song. He felt, like many listeners, that it made for a welcome break from the brassiness of the remainder of the band's second album. 'At times, *Against All Odds* can come off a little too cocksure, but Tulisa goes some way to redressing the balance on solo showcase "Comfortable", a heartfelt love song that provides a welcome break from all the bravado.' Like Balls, the website AllMusic's Jon O'Brien cast the band's doubters as out of touch with the younger generation. He concluded his own review of the album: 'Even though it's likely to alienate anyone who was born before the Phil Collins song of the same name, it's still a vibrant and hook-laden follow-up which is destined to be this year's back-of-the-school-bus soundtrack.'

As well as reviews, there had been a flurry of general news and gossip stories surrounding the release. It had been said that the band was going to record a song for the album with none other than Kylie Minogue. She was said to have approached them with the idea after hearing their debut album. 'Kylie really wants to surprise people. She is a big fan of what N-Dubz have been doing,' a source told the *Sun*. When an ITN journalist asked the band whether the rumour was true, Dappy almost walked away from the interview. 'We're getting asked this all the time,' he complained. However, it was a successful enough album without the queen of pop's involvement. Within a year they would add a third album to the shelves. In the meantime, they embarked on another tour. Although it was ostensibly to promote the album, they actually themed the tour more around Christmas. They visited 10 cities during the tour, which they budgeted themselves. They spent £100,000 on it and made back three times that. Smart business – they should try entering *The Celebrity Apprentice*. Dappy had, touchingly, spent much of the free time on the tour borrowing phones from people so he could call home and check on the wellbeing of his baby.

Tulisa's dedicated, workaholic tendencies had come to the fore again as they made the album and toured. She was determined to give it her all. Working night and day, resting fitfully at strange hours – the process quickly took a toll on her young body. She was not always eating perfectly and was not even taking vitamins or other health supplements to give her system a boost. With a 23-date live tour in front of thousands of fans, she became even more rundown and vulnerable. Soon, she became so exhausted that she decided to fly to Athens for a much needed rest. During the flight, she fainted. She received immediate medical attention and as soon as the plane landed in Greece she was taken to hospital amid fears that she had come down with swine flu, which was then spreading around the world. As she was examined by doctors in Pendeli, Jonathan Shalit told the Press Association Tulisa's band mates were 'all very worried about her'. He said that he had 'no idea how she got ill' but 'the nature of being a singer is that you meet and shake hands with a huge amount of people'.

The media had already become obsessed with the swine flu epidemic. With the opportunity to attempt a connection between the bug and the world of entertainment, little restraint was shown. IS THIS THE FIRST CELEBRITY SWINE FLU VICTIM? ran the headline in the *Daily Mail*. 'Chart-topping N-Dubz singer Tulisa in isolation ward with suspected case.' Within days she was given the all-clear on swine flu, and went to stay with her aunt in Greece. Despite not having swine flu, she was still very ill and weak. 'Hopefully she'll get better and be able to fly back towards the end of the week, but we don't know if she will be well enough,' her spokesman said. After she had recovered and flown home, she tried to laugh the entire episode off. 'At the end of the day it was just flu,' she wrote in *Against All Odds*. 'It *wasn't* swine flu! Thank you very much!' The scare story had guaranteed extra coverage for Tulisa and the band but she was uncomfortable with the hype that it generated.

Ironically, the following year *X Factor* judge Cheryl Cole – who Tulisa would in due course effectively replace on the talent show – would have a health scare of her own, which would be played out in front of television viewers on primetime Saturday evening television. She was filmed collapsing backstage during X Factor auditions and then disappeared from the public eye amid reports she was suffering from malaria.

There was yet more controversy in Tulisa's midst when her house was broken into by a serial crook in the summer. She was reportedly fuming with both her manager Shalit and Channel 4 after her £550,000 Watford property was featured on-screen during Being N-Dubz, despite her request that its location be concealed. Within days of the relevant episode being broadcast the break-in occurred. A Channel 4 spokesman defended the documentary makers, saying: 'It was a brief shot of the exterior, approved by N-Dubz management.' According to one report in the Sun, Tulisa had been left wondering whether she would now need to move house. Anthony Smith, 22, admitted breaking into her pad after a boozing and pill-popping session. Following his arrest, she responded in celebratory mood on her Twitter page. 'Ha ha they got the b*****d that did it! Calma is a bitch! All good I'm excited about buying my new apartment now! Life works in funny ways.' A series of blunders by Smith had made it simple for the police to catch him. He cut himself while entering Tulisa's home and left both blood and fingerprints everywhere. Her 60-inch plasma screen TV, for instance, was riddled with evidence. Although she was delighted to have learned that police had caught the burglar, she remained angry and shaken at the intrusion into her personal space.

What a different mood she had been in as she had celebrated her birthday just weeks before the break-in. As she turned 23 she sank plenty of champagne and then danced into the night at Ibiza's Pacha nightclub. One report claimed she was still partying at 7am – with her thong tied in her hair. Such wild behaviour earned her the approval of the *Sun*'s Gordon Smart, who announced he was considering her for his much discussed Caner Of The Year award for 2010. Her wild ways continued throughout the summer, with reports in the British tabloids that she was enjoying a rock'n'roll lifestyle as the band travelled America. Also while out in the United States, she had another tattoo done – this time she had the word Dappy inked on to her neck.

Meanwhile, there had been further singles released by N-Dubz. Their performance in the charts showed that Tulisa's band was gaining more and more fans. 'I Need You' reached No 5 in the UK charts, and 'Playing With Fire' got to No 14 (and UK No 3 in the R&B charts). The two singles they had released prior to those tracks had reached No 24 and No 64 – so the band was clearly on the up. Indeed, 'Playing With Fire' had reached No 15 on the strength of downloads alone, ahead of the physical release. The fabled kids at the back of the bus were busy downloading N-Dubz material. A further tour was embarked upon in the spring of 2010. They played 17 sell-out shows.

An insight into life on the road for the band was provided in their book *Against All Odds*. As 'the only chick' Tulisa admitted that life on the road was often far from fun for her. For that reason, she took to travelling separately from the boys. They took up residence in the tour bus for both travelling and – often – sleeping. However, she would follow in a car and would book hotels to sleep in. She had tried life on the tour bus but found it claustrophobic and motion sickness inducing. She described it as 'a smelly box' and in fairness one can only imagine the multitude of horrors produced by Dappy and co during long, boring times on motorways. She kept the boys at arm's length on the occasions that they did book a hotel. 'I make sure they're put on a different floor from me because I need to be away from them or I won't be getting any sleep.' The male members accept – and even understand – her wish to avoid the tour bus. They know their behaviour would frustrate her. In turn, they get frustrated by how long it takes her to get ready. Dappy has complained how she would even arrive late for recording sessions 'because she's doing her hair or something pointless'.

There are arguments within the band. All bands have them and with such feisty characters in N-Dubz, heated disagreements are inevitable. The rows they have are often about something Dappy or Fazer have done. 'It's very simple,' wrote Tulisa. She went on to explain that she just considers herself to be more mature than them, which is hard to argue with, particularly in her comparison to Dappy. She criticised him for behaviour she feels is inappropriate, such as clearly phasing out during an important interview. She said that angry words will often be exchanged during such fallings-out, with Fazer

Two sides of Tulisa – *left*, with mother Ann Byrne and, *below*, at the launch of her own perfume.

Above: Fazer, Tulisa and Dappy line up.

Below: N-Dubz at the Shepherds Bush Empire, London in 2009.

Right: Tulisa in N-Dubz mode at a beach festival in Weston-Super-Mare.

Below: Making an entrance at the 2010 Brit Awards in London.

Above: Tulisa never knowingly takes her eye off the ball – here at a celebrity football match in 2009.

Below: Dappy and Tulisa at the BBC Radio 1Xtra Live gig in London.

Above: Louis Walsh, Tulisa, Kelly Rowland and Gary Barlow making their presence known as judges on a certain TV talent show.

Below: In the mix with Tulisa's *X Factor* hopefuls Little Mix, from left: Leigh-Anne Pinnock, Jade Thirlwall, Tulisa herself, Jesy Nelson and Perrie Edwards.

Left: Proudly clutching both Gary Barlow and the Talent Show award won for the *X Factor* at the National Television Awards 2012.

Below: Tulisa in Manchester for the *X Factor*.

Tulisa with *X Factor* graduate Olly Murs at the Hammersmith Apollo in London.

occasionally taking her side. He often has to step in as the effective middleman between the two fiery cousins.

Mostly, though, she has found it is her against both of them. 'Our biggest issue and clash point is about the way we conduct ourselves,' she wrote. 'I like to be very professional whereas the boys don't really give a damn what people think.' She said she saw such an attitude as 'bad manners' and added that she did feel like 'a stressed mum trying to control them'. Behind this was a concern for herself. She felt that their misconduct 'rubs off' on her and how she is perceived. Fazer has said that the two cousins were always rowing during the band's active years due to her wish to be known as a 'grown-up mature woman' and Dappy's equally strong desire to remind her where she came from. For each time that Tulisa tried to play the part of a sophisticated young lady, Dappy was there to try and bring her – as he saw it – down to earth. She would clash with Fazer, too. Indeed, he remembers times that she would physically threaten him, saying: 'I'll knock you out right now!'

Tulisa's band faced controversy galore when Dappy texted a death threat to a Radio One listener. While they were being interviewed in the studio on the Chris Moyles Show, listeners began to send text messages to the studio. One, sent by 22-year-old Chloe Moody, declared that the band were 'losers' and singled out Dappy as 'vile' and 'a little boy with a silly hat'. Dappy noted down her number and tried to call her the following day. After she twice failed to pick up, he instead sent a fuming text message. It read: 'Your gonna die, U sent a very bad msg towards

N Dubz on The Chris Moyels show yesterday Morning and for that reason u will never be left alone!! If u say sorry I will leave u alone u ****.' When the puzzled Moody texted back to ask who was sending the message, he replied: 'Pick up the phone then u f****** Chicken'. A further text he sent read: 'u dum f****** ****head u can call me names over the radio but when I call u direct u chicken out u punk!nana f****** niiiii, Dappy.'

Moody was outraged, and told the *Sun*: 'It's terrifying when anybody sends you a death threat, whether it's real or not. Somebody of a fragile mind and nervous would be worrying what they were going to do. His behaviour is unprofessional. I'm considering going to the police.' She added: 'When you put yourself in the public eye you need to be able to handle criticism. I also feel let down by Radio One.' Her case against Radio One was tight – the station should not have allowed Dappy to see her number. Dappy apologised to both Moody and Radio One.

This controversy played out just months after Dappy had again embarrassed Tulisa's band when it first emerged that he had a conviction for assault after spitting in a girl's face. After a night drinking with a female fan he returned with her to her home in Chelmsford, Essex. There, he got into a row with two women, who called the police and Dappy was eventually to plead guilty to two counts of assault and received four weeks in jail, suspended for 12 months, and 100 hours' community service, to run concurrently, plus £50 compensation and £300 costs. At first the conviction was kept quiet. It was an embarrassing day for Tulisa when news of the incident reached the media. His subsequent behaviour following the Chris Moyles Show incident only made the discomfort more profound.

****

In June 2010, Tulisa was brought to the attention of a host of new people when she was featured on the Channel 4 series *Being... N-Dubz*. It was knowingly and huskily narrated by *Loose Women* favourite Lynda Bellingham. In the opening episode she introduced the band as 'a dynamite trio'. Tulisa and her band-mates wore 'head cams', which meant that the viewers could see life through their eyes. Dappy explained that while it took him and Fazer just five minutes to get ready in the morning, Tulisa took over two hours to handle 'the feminine side of things'. Meanwhile, the lady herself was shown being pampered at a flash hairdressing salon. She reflected that the 'stuff' she had to 'put up with' from her male band-mates is 'un-be*liev*able'. The show portrayed a deliberate contrast between her and the men of N-Dubz: while they take the tube to the studio, she is shown rolling-up in a flash, convertible car. 'Oh you donut – you diva,' shouts a mock-disgusted Dappy. She turned up two hours late to the Soccer Six celebrity football charity tournament, underscoring the 'diva' image the show was keen to promote.

When a pitch scrap broke out between Dappy, Fazer and rival rapper Lethal Bizzle, a breathless Tulisa was quick to weigh in. Addressing Lethal Bizzle's allegation that N-Dubz had stolen a song of his, she said: 'Let me pay a grand out of my pocket for a lie-detector test, bruv,' she said. 'But he don't wanna do it, why? Because he knows I'm telling the truth. Big-up N-Dubz!' Back in the football action she was the hero for her side when she scored the penalty that won her team the tournament. She celebrated with glee, parading the trophy, while an onlooking Dappy observed: 'Tulisa didn't do that bad after all!' While the insights into the band's day-to-day life were entertaining, in truth it was Dappy who stole the show throughout the series. He has a way with random wisecracks that play well in this format, though he – and the band and show in general – were not to everyone's taste. TV reviewer Keith Watson wrote in *Metro*: 'If you'd dropped in unannounced on *Being… N-Dubz*, you'd have sworn it was some kind of lame, MTV-style spoof … *Being… N-Dubz* was way funnier than any spoof because it was real. Well, as real as any show could hope to be that features cartoon characters called Dappy, Tulisa and Fazer.'

The *Scotsman*'s un-bylined review began by describing the band as an 'uncompromisingly stupid pop trio'. The reviewer was particularly harsh on Dappy, asking 'Seriously, what's wrong with him? Why doesn't he calm down? Half an hour of his incessant yammering, posturing and childish horseplay was enough to force me to abandon my liberal values and demand the return of national service.'

Tulisa soon took-part in a more sober and well received

television project. In the summer of 2010, Tulisa laid bare the truth of her mother's mental health issues in a BBC documentary called *Tulisa – My Mum And Me*. In it, she openly and movingly discussed her own experiences as the child of a mentally ill woman. She then takes to the road, interviewing other youngsters who have gone through similar experiences. 'I'm Tulisa, I'm probably best known to you for being the girl in N-Dubz, but there's a big part of my private life that I've always kept quiet about,' she said in the introduction. It was about to be thrust into the public eye, during the moving scenes that followed. She re-read old diaries of hers, including one from when she was 12 years old, in which she had declared that, for all her problems, she loved her mother 'with all my heart'. In another diary she had smeared her own blood onto the page to demonstrate that she had self-harmed. She then looked over old photographs, including some taken at Disneyland. Then Tulisa does a 'piece to camera' alone, recalling the full horrors she went through as a child, including the police arriving to section her mother, who was 'literally restrained and dragged away'. She explains how she was haunted by a 'vivid image' of her mother 'screaming in an ambulance'. She revisits the hospital her mother had been taken to, and recalled how her mother seemed so 'defeated'. Tulisa had wanted to ask her mother what was going on, but she realised that her mother – not her – was almost the child in this situation.

Tulisa then visits other children who have faced comparable horrors. This starts with a girl called Mia from

Windsor, whose mother Tanya suffered from bipolar disorder. The rapport between Tulisa and 16-year-old Mia was palpable. Despite coming from a different background, Tulisa related to the challenges. She also visited 15-year-old Hannah from Dover, who had suffered as a result of the clinical depression of her mother Julie. The anger that Hannah admitted she had felt was something Tulisa very much understood. Like the younger Tulisa, Hannah said she had turned to cannabis to deal with the pain. She left Dover concerned for Hannah and Julie, who had seemed far less tranquil than the Windsorian family she visited. She then spoke with people closer to home. First, her best friend from school Mercedes, and then the N-Dubz DJ Mazer, who told her how he remembered her behaviour when she was 13. 'You were a bit crazy, T, to tell the truth,' he said. He also speculated that without the direction music gave her, he thought she would be 'Probably in a council flat with twins, signing on'. He added: 'It would not have been a good look, man.'

Later in the programme, introducing young carers to a network of support groups, Tulisa took Hannah to a specialist youth group. In doing so, she followed the narrative of many N-Dubz songs: be unflinchingly honest about a dark situation and then search out the positive light you can bring to it. 'Small improvements can make a huge difference when you're struggling as a young carer,' said Tulisa. She also revisited Mia in Windsor, who had just sat her GCSE exams. As Tulisa reminded the viewers, she personally had never sat her GCSEs, leaving school at 15.

An issue that increasingly troubled Tulisa during the making of the programme was one that had haunted her for some time. She was scared that her mother's health issues had begun in her late teens but had only really started to show themselves in her early twenties. 'I've always suspected that mental illness runs in families and that my chances of getting ill are greater than other people's because of what Mum has.' So she visited Cardiff University, where a huge study into such theories was being undertaken. To what extent, she wanted to know as she donned her lab coat, did genes play in an individual's susceptibility to mental illness?Having heard an explanation from Professor Nick Craddock, she cut straight to the point. 'So... is mental illness hereditary?' she asked.

'Well, yes,' he replied, adding that there is a tendency for it to run in families.

She then went further, wondering whether she was susceptible to getting mentally ill. So she underwent a psychiatric interview by Professor Craddock. She explained to him about her panic attacks, self-harming and suicide attempts.

'It's clear that you ... have had depression, and that means you're susceptible in the future to have more depressions,' he told her. So far, so obvious. He added: 'What I would say is that in anyone who's had panics or been low it's really important to look after your health –

both your physical health and obviously your mental health.' He advised her to avoid triggers that might risk further mental issues. He told her to avoid drugs, excessive drinking or irregular sleep patterns.

None of this seemed to be rocket science, yet Tulisa admitted that what he had told her had 'really freaked me out'. In fairness, she reflected that she now realised she had a susceptibility to mental illness and a lifestyle that put her at risk. She added that it was a 'dramatic jump' to move from considering herself as having a one in a hundred chance to a one in ten chance of becoming mentally ill. It had been a harsh realisation for Tulisa. She said: 'The risk of me ever suffering from mental illness, that is quite a lot for me to take on board. I'm not sure if I'm pushing myself to the limit at times.'

However, she explained, that at the end of a live show she felt that the crash of adrenaline after she came off stage was akin to a 'comedown'. She added: 'I do get this feeling of emptiness....Sometimes I end up feeling quite lonely.' The show left Tulisa setting up her first house. She said that she had realised that she had 'shut off' feelings about the troubles of her past. 'I guess it's just been a journey for me to move on and accept the situation and deal with it,' she said. As Ann arrived to see her daughter's first house, Tulisa was proud to show her – and the viewers – the spare room she had set up especially for her mum to sleep in. 'Oh, Tula,' said Ann, with moving pride. She concluded the programme predicting that she would always be a carer for her mum. 'Being a young carer never stops,' she said.

The press reaction to Tulisa's documentary was very positive. Scribes who might not normally have much positive to say about her often expressed admiration at this other side of her. 'As with many BBC3 documentaries about "issues", it's been made with a young audience in mind, but Tulisa is an honest and compassionate host,' wrote the *Guardian*'s Julia Raeside. The *Independent*'s Simmy Richman said Tulisa's 'warmth, honesty and approachability meant [she] came across as a sort of urban Princess Di, reaching out to people society might otherwise sweep under its carpet.' However, as she had suspected would happen, there was indeed scepticism over her decision to go public about her mother's issues. Some claimed that it was an exploitative publicity stunt. One online viewer quipped that she had made the programme purely as 'a bid to generate some good karma for when she meets the man upstairs'. James Steiner's review on the On The Box television website went further, saying: 'It is a shame that Tulisa could not tame the media-hungry-whore that dwells inside every celebrity as she resorts to several shameless plugs of her band.' This is a nonsensical sentiment, as her fame was a key part of the appeal of the programme to the channel and its viewers. Back in the mainstream, the *Radio Times* called her programme: 'A brave, eye-opening, and...potentially life-changing film'. The *Times* felt that Tulisa's programme had single-handedly given the channel a fresh lease of life. 'What a service the once derided BBC Three does for its target audience (and me) by using celebrity to open eyes to the awful variety of teenage experience.'

As the media began to discuss her mother's experiences and the issue in general, Tulisa was at pains to leave the matter on a positive and loving note. 'Mental healthcare in this country is much better now, although we still have a long way to go,' she said. 'Too often people like me are just left to get on with it. But there are support groups for young carers now, which is a huge step forward because one of the worst things about dealing with my mum was how helpless and alone I felt at such a vulnerable age.' Mindful that her documentary and the motivations behind it might be misinterpreted, she wanted people to know that she and her mother have a relationship that is normal and loving in the important ways. 'No matter what has happened, I love my mum,' she said. 'She is happy for my success and I feel that for the first time in years I can have a more relaxed relationship with her.'

She added that her mother has improved since the darker days of old. 'I'm not sure if it was a combination of better understanding of mental illness, better community care or that my mum just struck lucky with the doctors, but finally they realised that her medication wasn't working,' said Tulisa, explaining how things began to turn around. As a result, her issues were examined in a new light. 'They completely re-evaluated her case and she was diagnosed as having both bipolar and schizophrenia,' she said. 'Now she takes drugs to combat both. She's good at taking them and for the most part she has been stable. There are times when she'll say mad things. I'm in the middle of decorating the house and I had a bottle of white spirit in one of the rooms. When she saw I'd left a lighter nearby she started freaking out because she was convinced something dreadful would happen. But I can tell her to calm down and we can laugh about it now, whereas before it would have led to an argument. There are times when I get frustrated by her behaviour but at least now I have the space and freedom to escape from it. I believe a lot of it comes down to how strong you are mentally. I have been through a lot for someone my age but it has made me strong and determined and I have to pray that is enough for me not to suffer the way my mum has.' The final word from Tulisa on the matter: 'They say blood is thicker than water and it's true.' Amen.

At the end of November 2010, N-Dubz released their third studio album. Titled *Love.Live.Life*, it was to be their most successful release to date. The lead single for the album had been released in May – it was not just arguably the band's finest hour but also surely Tulisa's finest vocal performance. 'We Dance On' begins with the emotional strings of Pachelbel's 'Canon in D Major', a beginning reminiscent of 'Dry Your Eyes' by The Streets. It is only when Dappy's chant heralds the house backing track that the N-Dubz stamp is put upon it. Tulisa then launches straight into the vocals. The vocals warn that tough and challenging times are ahead, but Tulisa promises that she will be OK and promises to break any obstacles placed in front of her.

With the underdog card played, the second N-Dubz favourite theme is introduced in the chorus, when the band declare that everything will be all right. Positive unity in the face of adversity – this was brilliant, vintage N-Dubz stuff. The house music duo Bodyrox collaborated on the fine backing track, making this a magnificent three minutes and seven seconds of music. With dancing placed as a metaphor for facing the challenges life throws at us, this was almost an urban, 21st-century twist on the 1930s big-band song 'Let's Face The Music And Dance'. It was also compared in theme by two critics to the sort of message reggae star Bob Marley would impart. 'Like a big bowl of chicken soup, this leaves you feeling warm, fuzzy and generally a bit better inside,' said Digital Spy. Too right it does. From Tulisa's personal perspective, the most pleasing critical response to the song came in the *Mirror*, where Gavin Martin wrote: 'Often forced to take a back seat while her male counterparts lead, N-Dubz' front lady Tulisa comes out front for this crowd-pleasing and unifying floor filler with a hint of classical spice.'

Perhaps the final word on this remarkable moment in Tulisa's band's career should go to BBC website critic Fraser McAlpine, who accurately placed the song's message in the context of the lives of Tulisa, Dappy and Fazer, as well as admitting it brought him to tears listening to it. 'They know they have the strength to get through the bad times, because they have already had to find this out, the hard way. And so long as they've got each other to rely on, the way they always have, well there's nothing they can't do...' It reached No 6 in the UK singles chart. With such a great lead single, optimism and expectation were high for their forthcoming third album. Before that hit the shops a second single from it was released, called 'Best Behaviour', which we will discuss below.

The album was released in collaboration between Island Records and All Around The World. It had been reported that Island Def Jam boss LA Reid – a hugely successful and influential music industry figure – had become a big fan of the band and was keen to sign them. It was reported that he rolled out the red carpet for the band in America, arranging helicopter trips and plush meals. The Island Def Jam A&R man Max Gousse announced that a deal had been struck with the band. He said: 'I signed N-Dubz because they're great entertainers and speak to London's youth unlike any other band. We want to bring their message to the rest of the world.' No wonder Gousse was proud of the deal – it had been he who had first brought the act to attention of Reid and the other label bosses. Fazer spoke for himself, Tulisa and Dappy when he said: 'Getting a US deal is something we've been working towards for a while and we can't wait to get out to the States and have our music heard globally.'

The band found they had a clash of cultures with their new producers when it came to their liberal use of certain British slang terms. 'We worked with some massive names: Jean Baptiste, who works with Black Eyed Peas, Salaam Remi, who does a lot of Amy Winehouse's stuff, and Jim Jonsin, who worked on Beyoncé's last album,' said Dappy in an interview with the *Daily Star*. 'And to be honest it was tough at times trying to get our lingo across to them.

We were saying stuff like: "I swear down, man", but they didn't know what we were talking about. They didn't like the slang and tried to get us to talk proper English. We got our vocab up to scratch a bit but we also said to them: "We come from the country that made the English language, just trust us." We put our creative foot down and in the end lost none of our Englishness.' He was in ebullient mood – even making the boastful claim that the prestigious American producers had eventually deferred to him and his male band mate. 'Me and Fazer do all the post-production on our records – the arrangement, the beats, the mixing. We take it from a demo to the finished product,' he said. 'We couldn't stand aside even when working with those big American guys. In the end they said to us: "You know what, you guys might as well sit at the desk and do it yourselves." That was great to hear.'

The album begins with a short track called 'Intro'. After Dappy has made some rather half-baked remarks about life in Baghdad, Basra and other hard-hit areas, the song rather fades away. It is not an opener in the class of *Against All Odds'* intro. 'Best Behaviour' begins by dealing with the highs and lows of touring and the feeling when the act returns home to normality at the end of it. Here, the band cries out for the stability of a real love. Tulisa is again on strong vocal form, singing about how she cried on the floor of an empty room following a tour. The song develops into a decent indictment of a feeling that plagues many live performers: what is the use of being cheered by thousands of audience members if there is not that special one person to love you when the curtain goes down. It is a gentle enough song, but it takes a more intense angle when the lyrics warn of 'danger' if a partner is not found soon. Tulisa sings emotionally as the song comes towards its end.

For the next track, 'Took It All Away', it is as if the band have worried that all that yearning for love in 'Best Behaviour' had shown a bit too much sensitivity. So in 'Took It All Away', Dappy is soon admitting to a number of infidelities with girls. Tulisa is fuming in her lyrics, calling Dappy a 'traitor', and leaving him complaining that she responded with such anger. She taunts him that it is now her who is flirting with others. In 'Living For The Moment', Tulisa sings about her own life, in a cramped council flat with her mother, and how she was the one that had to save them. It might not seem the most positive of songs, and one that sees Dappy drop numerous F-bombs. However, the ultimate message is that listeners should let go of anything that has bothered them in their past and instead live for the moment. For Tulisa this was a particularly pertinent message. Anyone who knew of her past would consider her well placed to deliver this message.

A similar message is delivered in 'Love Live Life', the next track. However, this time it is delivered in a more positive – and certainly more commercial – fashion. The song is in part a throwback to the house sounds of the late 1980s, when the band members were scarcely alive. In 'Scream My Name', the band speak about the experiences of fame. With its references to Twitter and YouTube, as well as its sense of a star who wants to be loved, it is in a way – and N-Dubz fans may like to avert their eyes for a moment – almost like a Justin Bieber song. It is certainly narcissism at its finest.

'Love Sick' is one for the ladies, in which Tulisa and Lady NY sing about how the romantic hopes and expectations of the fairer sex are not always matched by the realities of life. Although Tulisa did not write the lyrics, they reflect well the experiences she had with many guys earlier in life. Again, a positive message comes out in the end. Although she does not appear in 'Toot It And Boot It', the song remains relevant to Tulisa. Many women – even those who do not self-define as feminists – would be uncomfortable with some of the lyrics and imagery of songs like this. Whether Tulisa's 'feisty' image is compromised or in fact strengthened by the fact that she is in a musical genre that frequently refers to women in less than flattering terms is a matter of taste. The question is resolved in part later in the album.

He and Fearless later trade lyrics of fury aimed at an unnamed wannabe act who worked hard for fame but never achieved it, in contrast to their own sincerity and success. It's an angry song that takes no prisoners and spares no blushes. In 'So Alive', Skepta guests. In the promotional video he rather dwarfs the band. That said, Tulisa looks magnificent in her white outfit. The lyrics of the chorus again encourage listeners to hold their hands up to the sky. In the second verse, Tulisa attempts to show the world who the real (female) boss is. She then boasts that she drives men crazy, as they all wish she was theirs. Tulisa also says that she is earning more money than any of the men who fancy her. It is her answer to those who doubted how she existed in such a macho world as urban music. It might not be enough for all observers, some of whom will just say that she is the subject of male domination. However, in this song the female boss is in no doubt over where she stands. In 'Cold Shoulder', she shares the lyrics with Dappy as they each beckon a lover to spend a passionate night with them. Again, she stands here on equal terms with the men of the world.

In 'Morning Star', the band goes all romantic on us. Both Tulisa and Dappy show hitherto rarely demonstrated sensitive sides. The lyrics even hint at the classic soul song 'Wishing On A Star'. This is a song about a special someone and the love that can be shared with them, rather than about hump 'em and dump 'em encounters, as many of their other songs have been. Tulisa pleads with the man not to go. Given its late place in the album's track list, N-Dubz are also sending that message to their fans. There is still more they want to show the fans, they are saying. Little could anyone have known as the album was released quite how long it would be until such demonstrations would begin.

The outro then brings album to a theatrical close. Again, we have the bookend theme, as in *Against All Odds*. Except here we get the addition of the aforementioned triumph that is 'We Dance On'. Given the indefinite hiatus N-Dubz are on at the time of going to press, perhaps this song is a fitting closing message.

In the *Daily Mirror*, Gavin Martin said Tulisa and co were 'boisterous' and 'upbeat'. However he added that the quality 'wavers' and gave the album just three out of five stars. The *Evening Standard*'s David Smyth gave it the same score, and complained that: 'They're in too much of a hurry to develop their frantic, hip-pop sound.' Perhaps the most positive part of his review came in passing: he described the band as 'rising fast towards national institution status'. For Andy Gill of the *Independent*, the album was mostly 'fairly predictable fare'. Awarding it three stars, he nonetheless said 'So Alive' is 'blessed with an ebullient bonhomie which, despite the lingering attitude, proves engagingly infectious.' Killian Fox of the *Observer* wrote that the album: 'sees the Camden trio blowing the spoils of their success on Gucci and champagne' and complained that 'the insistence on having fun soon wears thin'.

It was Caroline Sullivan of the *Guardian* who spotlighted Tulisa's place in the collection. 'If they sound transatlantic, their lyrics are still quintessentially British, especially on "Living for the Moment" … Their teen audience will love it; adults may find it all too frantic.' Again, she awarded the album three out of five stars. *Metro*, too, focused on our heroine's contribution to that song, declaring that: 'Singer Tulisa takes an appealingly spirited turn on "Living For The Moment" and there's something oddly endearing about the boundless enthusiasm of N-Dubz for enjoying a life they've grafted hard for.' It was slightly guarded praise, but praise nonetheless.

Which is more than could be said for the review of the

Scotsman. It began by saying of Dappy that he is 'a rapper who makes Flavor Flav look like Stephen Hawking' and said the band had 'never been taken as seriously' as acts such as Tinie Tempah. 'Even with the occasional sweary word, it's still just kids' stuff,' concluded Fiona Shepherd, giving it just two stars. Fraser McAlpine also took aim at Dappy, writing in the *NME* that he is 'a self-righteous storm in a tea cosy'. He gave the album five out of 10 stars, saying: 'This is, of course, both crackers and compelling, like a philosophy lecture in a chimps' tea party.' Plenty of record buyers were happy to give the tea party a chance. *Love.Live.Life* reached UK No 7 and an exciting UK No 3 in the RnB chart. At the time of writing, it is the last N-Dubz album to be released. Tulisa would now move to new areas – and her fame would rocket.

****

Before she decided it was 'time..to face...the muusssic' of *The X Factor*, Tulisa had another stab at acting. She took the part of Amber in a British horror film called *Demons Never Die*. It follows the knock-on effect that a suicide has on a group of friends. Other people to act in it included *Misfits* star Robert Sheehan, *Hollyoaks*' Emma Rigby and *Hustle* actor Ashley Walters. For Tulisa, this was a break into a new part of the arts world and one she welcomed. Since watching films such as *Tomb Raider* and *Resident Evil* she had been keen to get into the world of acting. 'The movie's got that urban twist, but it's also very dark,' she said. As such, it had one foot firmly in one of Tulisa's favourite cinematic genres, with an original and refreshing twist. 'I love urban films, but it's nice to be able to combine urban with something else and I think this is the first to be able to do that; here it's not just revolving around urban life; it's actually got a plot within urban life.'

'The character I play is a pretty dark one – very on edge and unstable. It seems she's like that because of a boy, so it's not too hard to relate to! I remember when I was 15 years old, but she's a bit psychotic and has a lot of issues going on. It's all about this suicide that's happened and why it's happened.' Although Tulisa's acting experience was not particularly deep at the time, she knew enough from past acting ventures to evaluate and appreciate how helpful it was for her to be playing a part of someone who had been through similar experiences to her. 'It's always easier to play a character if you've experienced those issues yourself. Obviously she's quite depressed and when I was a kid I went through certain issues; so it was easier to get in to that mode.' On a lighter note, she said: 'I've always wanted to do a real kicking butt role. A bit of a Lara Croft, *Tomb Raider*... I love the *Resident Evil* character. Being able to learn a fighting skill and having to do training... just beating people up and I've got guns in holsters on my thighs which I pull out.'

As she looked ahead in 2010, Tulisa had no clue how much her career and life was about to change the following year. After dismissing *The X Factor* and the easy route to fame it gave to acts that she often did not rate, she said that her ambition was something far more mundane. Indeed, her biggest wish for the months ahead was actually something that many people would run a mile from – a vision of domestic DIY hell and the retail torture that comes with it. 'All I want, my ambition for this year is to just get my house and spend a month decorating it,' she said. 'I'm really excited. I can't wait. I want to go to IKEA and do a whole day there from like 8 o'clock in the morning... it's all I've been thinking about.' She had set out a far grander ambition in the closing pages of *Against All Odds*. She wrote: 'In 10 years' time I want to be right at the top. Simple as. That's why we're going to America. It's scary as it means starting from scratch all over again. It's a whole new market and I'm scared but excited. This is the new thing for me now. I've set myself a new goal and I'm going to work at it – because I like a challenge to keep me mentally stimulated.'

As it happened, 2011 would see a whole new challenge for her that would keep her not so much mentally stimulated as obsessed to the point of exhaustion. She had come to the attention of one of the entertainment world's biggest players – nothing would ever be the same again for Tulisa.

CHAPTER
SEVEN

At the end of May 2011, following much speculation, Tulisa was confirmed as one of the new judges for *The X Factor*. Finally allowed to share this exciting news publicly, she sent out a lively message on Twitter. 'Very excited about joining the X Factor. Ive always loved the show and I want to thank you all for supporting me....' [sic] She added: 'On my journey this far, rest assured the Tulisa you know isn't going anywhere. I don't no how to be anything other than myself... & thats what I'll be. I hope I can bring that raw in your face, real element 2 the show (& the warmth/love cus you know I'm a softy at heart).' [sic]

Meanwhile, she and N-Dubz had played what was described as their final concert 'for the foreseeable future'. They had taken by this stage to arriving on stage on motorbikes, dressed sharply all in black. 'Considering the group are new to arenas, it was a smooth affair, though after a while it dragged a bit,' wrote Tim Burrows in the *Daily Telegraph*, acknowledging nonetheless that the audience loved it. Afterwards, the band got stuck into the backstage refreshments. As a hung over Dappy said the following day: 'We got off stage and the beers were flat, so I started drinking it like water.' The first morning of the rest of his life was spent vomiting into the toilet before setting off for an interview with the *Guardian* newspaper. All far from ideal from his point of view.

As well as playing this bookending gig, the band also parted company from Def Jam. There had been creative differences between band and label. Though Tulisa put the case to her band mates for them to continue the relationship, it came to an end in the summer. Trying to put a positive spin on the story, Dappy told the *Mirror*: 'They might say they've dropped us but we were never going to co-operate with them when they decided to change what we are. If we had co-operated we would still be signed. Tulisa thought we should do it because we could make some money out of it, but I said no. For them to say they dropped us makes me angry because we just didn't want to change who we are or what we do.'

A more measured, official statement from the band's management stated: 'N-Dubz have left the Def Jam imprint in the USA due to creative differences over musical direction. This was 100 per cent the band's decision and they remain signed to Universal worldwide.' There was talk that Tulisa had – as part of the parting of the ways –

signed a solo deal with Island Records, which contained a clause that gave Def Jam first refusal on American rights. However, her solo effort would have to wait until she had fulfilled her *X Factor* duties for the entire series. Indeed, the question of whether she would even merit a solo career rather depended on the success – or otherwise – of her first *X Factor* series.

Their American travels had been documented on the second series of *Being...N-Dubz*, which was broadcast on Channel 4 in the spring of 2011, as Tulisa was waiting for her *X Factor* duties to commence. Initially, Tulisa and Fazer jet out to America, leaving Dappy to fight off a bout of illness in the UK. They watch Tinie Tempah perform and then link up with Dappy in Los Angeles. Tulisa attends a Def Jam party, which had been snubbed by her two band-mates – another instance of their differing approach to their careers. Elsewhere, Tulisa is mistaken for a cast member of the US television show *Jersey Shore*, and she is shown attending yet another beauty salon, in keeping with the 'diva of the band' image the series had tried to paint of her. In another segment they are shown at a shooting range – though Tulisa says she doesn't like guns. It was not world-changingly insightful stuff, but was entertaining enough. The *Mirror* said that this series showed a different N-Dubz, an N-Dubz that 'say cute things like 'clumsy clogs, clumsy clogs' when they accidentally spill their hot chocolate and like goofing around in swimming pools.' The Holy Moly website was bitchiness defined when, at the end of its preview of episode one, it broke with the usual convention of listing transmission details in italics at the foot of the article. Instead, it declared: '*Being N-Dubz is on telly, but we're not telling you where or when, because nobody should watch it, because it is shit and will make you grind your teeth to dust.*'

As we have seen, the fears and disagreements that hit the band after it was dropped by Def Jam were not the only concerns that arose in the wake of Tulisa's *X Factor* announcement. There was concern in the N-Dubz camp that by joining such a mainstream branch of the entertainment industry as *The X Factor*, Tulisa was turning her back on not just the band but the entire ethos that made N-Dubz so attractive to its millions of fans. She realised that she needed to respond to these fears immediately, and added a follow-up message on Twitter, in which she directly addressed the N-Dubz fans. 'I can't wait to find the next star of the UK,' she continued. 'I am still a member of NDubz & they will b my team till the day I die. People that dont know r story can never understand the way u guys do how important r loyalty is as a band to us ... The Female Boss is ready to rumble. BRING IT ON!!!! Xxx'

All the same, Tulisa's carefully cultivated 'street' image was something she would need to fight hard to hold on to as she underwent an inevitable transformation for *The X Factor*. She had offered a personal style guide to readers of the official N-Dubz book, in which she spoke of 'slobbing about' in lounge wear, including Adidas trainers, velour tracksuits with her hair scraped back and minimal make-up. Her favourite shopping locations were Brent Cross shopping centre, Kilburn High Street and Camden High Street. She said: 'I don't really buy anything that costs over 50 quid, except maybe trainers.' As an *X Factor* judge, she would be expected to wear outfits that cost a lot more than '50 quid'. Indeed, she would be under pressure to accept the dictates of the show's in-house style team. The media has for many years become obsessed with playing female *X Factor* judges off against one another, with weekly 'style wars' assessments of the outfits of past rival judges such as Cheryl Cole and Dannii Minogue a staple part of the middle-market newspaper and celebrity weeklies' coverage of the ITV show. Perhaps the line in her own previous style guide that would most chime with the *X Factor* ethos was 'I believe in looking classy 100 per cent'. That gave hope for some common ground as she prepared to join the judging panel of Britain's leading show.

The opportunities that opened for her as an *X Factor* judge far outweighed the challenges. Indeed, for her, it felt liberating to be able to style herself as a standalone individual, rather than a member of a three-piece band. 'Being in N-Dubz I was constantly having to accommodate the two band-mates either side of me,' she told *Star* magazine. 'I couldn't wear the things I wanted to because it wasn't ghetto enough for the group's look.' She was immediately being spoken of as the 'new Cheryl Cole' – and it certainly seemed that she had been chosen to fill Cole's shoes. Like the Geordie Girls Aloud star, Tulisa was the youngest of the new panel and was also expected to be the feistiest. Cole, through the success she made of herself on *The X Factor*, became the nation's sweetheart. Was it even feasible that Tulisa of N-Dubz could do the same? Did she want to? There was so much to see.

It was all change for the 2011 series. Simon Cowell – busy launching *The X Factor USA* – was absent, and both Cole and Minogue had flown the nest too. Only Louis Walsh from the previous season remained. The head judge would be Take That star Gary Barlow, who trousered a reported £1.5million when he signed up. He was no stranger to Tulisa: she had actually spoken about Barlow in the N-Dubz book, *Against All Odds*. She described him as 'chilled out', adding 'probably too chilled in fact'. She recalled songwriting sessions she had with Barlow in which his laidback nature meant they fell asleep. 'But he is soooo talented,' she added. She also spoke of how they would 'crack open a few beers and have a curry'. As well as admiring his talent, she was also enthralled by how down-to-earth he came across to her. 'He doesn't behave like a big superstar at all,' she said. Even Dappy called Barlow 'a good lad.'

Whether their existing friendship played a part in one of them recommending the other for a place on the panel is not clear. Indeed, it had been rumoured at one stage that Tulisa had failed an audition to join the *X Factor* panel due to her repeated use of foul language. 'Tulisa did do a one-hour audition but was turned down because she couldn't stop swearing,' a source had reportedly told a newspaper. 'It was all the time and bosses became worried about putting her on live TV in front of millions of viewers, including children. If she ended up cursing or making a rude comment live on the show, the programme would get into serious trouble.' Tulisa later dismissed the entire suggestion, but controversy would never be far away.

As her fame rocketed, she naturally gave more interviews to the press. In a brief example she named the exclusive clothing lines of Vivienne Westwood and Alexander McQueen, and then the high street brands River Island and Lipsy. Other brands she named included the Nando's chicken restaurant chain, the energy drink Red Bull, make-up company Rimmel and the fashionable Ugg boot range. These interviews and Tulisa's cheeky persona during them were certainly getting her noticed.

One interview from the past that Tulisa might prefer people to forget was the one she gave in 2010, when she launched a scathing attack on *The X Factor* and the acts it had launched. She was asked if she found it frustrating, after all the work she had put into her own career, to see reality television acts rocket to fame so quickly and comparatively easily. 'Yeah, it's annoying,' she told RTE Ten. 'It's annoying watching them just come up there and become worldwide acts selling millions of records after just standing in a queue for an hour. It happens overnight to them.' She then said that she had concluded that it was not worth getting upset about the issue, before adding a closing dig at the reality television genre, saying: 'And half of those acts, if they came out off their own bat and not on *X Factor*, wouldn't sell ten records so then you've just got to remind yourself of that.'

Indeed, it was an interview dominated by damnation of fame and the industry that supports it. The God-fearing Tulisa even went as far as saying she would pray for forgiveness, such was her claimed revulsion for the celebrity circus. 'Sometimes I feel like I'm sinning,' she said. 'I ask God for forgiveness. I'm like "God forgive for being in such a silly, shallow industry," because it's based on giving other people power and putting other people up and letting other people look up to them. It makes them feel like they're below them.'

It is worth pausing to consider where Tulisa was in her life and career at this stage. A young woman in her twenties, with her band's best days perhaps behind them, she inevitably attracted comparisons between her position and that of Cheryl Cole when she had first joined the *X Factor* judging panel. These comparisons are interesting given that Tulisa ostensibly – if not officially – replaced Cole on the panel. Cole was 25 when she was hired by *The X Factor*. She was famous through her membership of girl band Girls Aloud and due to her tumultuous love life and infamous due to her conviction for assault occasioning actual bodily harm, following a scrap in a nightclub toilet in 2003. She had yet to formally separate from her husband Ashley Cole, had not embarked on her solo career, and also, more crucially, had yet to be crowned the 'nation's sweetheart'. In other words she was famous, but it is important to recall just how much her fame and popularity rocketed as a result of her *X Factor* exposure.

Tulisa, at 23 two years younger than Cole had been as

her *X Factor* experience began, could eye Cole's experiences with a mixture of hope and caution. The rewards for being part of the *X Factor* judging panel clearly go beyond the specific exposure and renumeration. The scale of those rewards is variable, though. There is no automatic golden path for any *X Factor* judge. In this sense, the situation is similar for the judges and acts. For every Leona Lewis, Olly Murs and One Direction there are plenty of Leon Jacksons and Steve Brooksteins – winners who flopped despite topping the vote on such a popular show. Likewise, though Cole had made the most of her exposure as an *X Factor* judge, it is undeniable that other reality television judges such as Dannii Minogue, Ellen DeGeneres and others had benefited far less.

One can add into the comparison between Tulisa and Cole two additional variables. Firstly, Cole had emerged from the reality television genre herself. Girls Aloud were formed during 2002's series *Popstars: The Rivals*. Therefore, she always carried that inherent sense of being 'the people's champion' who had been democratically elected to fame. Secondly, as Tulisa scarcely had her feet under the *X Factor* table she was shown what a fickle beast it can be when Cole was unceremoniously dumped from her judging role on *The X Factor USA*. Cowell had felt she did not fit into the show as he nervously launched it in America. This was a crushing blow for Cole who had left the UK series and her home country in general to follow her hope of becoming a true star in America. The immediate effect on Tulisa of Cole's humiliation was a sustained onslaught of media speculation that Cole would return to the UK panel at her expense. More generally, the episode reminded the canny Tulisa that all the foundations of a successful celebrity career are tenuous. She felt more determined than ever to enjoy the moment and to make the most of this golden opportunity that had come her way. She approached the series with the blessing of Cole, though some press reports portrayed the two young women as sworn enemies, secretly loathing one another. Indeed, it was the blessing of Cole that helped Tulisa find the strength to face the tribulations that came with it. 'I could have become Britain's most hated woman by replacing her, but having her support made all the difference,' she told *Heat*. 'She told me there was no bitterness and I should go for it. That made me a lot more relaxed.'

The official promotional trailers for the 2011 series, introducing Tulisa and the other new judges to the public, were typically boisterous *X Factor* stuff. In one, a clip was shown of Tulisa animatedly asking a contestant 'Are you mental?' When the first episode hit the airwaves, her opening words to the viewers were to announce she had joined the panel because she is 'young and current'. As one newspaper reviewer observed the next day, by that she could have meant that her predecessor Cole was neither. She admitted she was 'dreading' the first slot of auditions, so nervous was she about what lay ahead. The first thing she noticed was the pressure that comes from the audience members behind her. She soon settled in and made a success of things. Indeed, she was for many viewers the very cream of the new panel, as Britain's top entertainment series entered the unimaginable – life after Simon Cowell.

The first act shown auditioning in the opening episode of the series was 18-year-old Frankie Cocozza. The mop-haired singer presented himself as a bit of a wild child and 'a liability' in his opening VT. Asked why he was auditioning he said, 'I just want to be famous.' He said, 'The lady judges might get a couple of winks if they're lucky,' and he certainly grabbed Tulisa's attention on-stage when he said he had the names of seven girls tattooed on his bum. She checked she had heard him correctly, then added: 'How about – I don't believe you?' He dutifully turned his back on the audience and flashed his backside so all could see the tattoos. Tulisa and the rest of the panel were in hysterics. Walsh asked Cocozza whether, if the panel put him through, Cocozza would have Tulisa and Kelly's names tattooed on his butt. 'If they pay for it,' he quipped. His rocky performance of 'Valerie' was enough to see Cocozza through to the next round. As it would transpire, the opening act would become synonymous with the entire series, even after his premature exit.

Other notable acts to appear in the opening episode included the 48-year-old Hong Kong-born Tai Chi instructor Goldie Cheung, who was shown vomiting just before her audition, which turned into a madcap performance. Kitty Brucknell told the panel she was 26 and then gave an overall performance that positioned her as the needy and slightly unnerving contestant of the series, in the model of Katie Waissel the previous year. The most talented of the openers was Northern Ireland teenager Janet Devlin, whose sweet and quirky rendition of 'Your Song' had the entire venue enchanted. Tulisa's responses to these key figures in the opening episode were: to Goldie: 'She's so refreshing – I'm sold!'; to Kitty she said: 'You've got a very quirky personality, people will either love you or hate you'; she told Janet 'I love the fact you're so shy, it's so endearing – that is a recording vocal.'

There had been concern and even suspicion among many faithful X Factor viewers that the new panel would not work. However, on the evidence of the opening show there was much to admire in the selection. While Barlow had been more animated – and certainly harsher – than his previously slightly dour media image had suggested, and Rowland's soulful American patter went down a treat, it was for many viewers Tulisa who was the revelation among the new faces. She certainly brought some feistiness to proceedings but she had not been the lippy, out-of-control kid that some people had feared she would be. Instead, she had balanced her youthful, urban image with that of a mature, graceful twentysomething who was on the show on merit and, crucially, believed herself to be so.

One contestant in the opening show had not been quite so convinced of Tulisa's charms. George Gerasimou had auditioned in 2009 in a three-piece band called Triple Trouble. They turned out to be well named, as they reacted furiously to criticism from Simon Cowell. They slammed their microphones to the floor and stormed off stage. Gerasimou said that he would not be a 'clown' and insisted that as he had matured, he would be able to cope with any criticism from the judges, however negative. However, his song performance was below average and his newfound maturity consequently got put to the test afterwards. He appeared horrified that the judges had called for the backing track to be stopped. Then the audience began to chant 'Off! Off! Off!' which did nothing to improve his mood.

Rowland and Barlow both criticised him, with the latter saying that far from maturing like a good wine or cheese, the singer had matured 'like a bad curry, mate'. Tulisa then said that she felt he had not changed his attitude at all. 'I felt a lot of aggression off you, you're very angry,' she said. He replied that he was a 'puppy' and that he was being misjudged. 'It's not a good vibe,' Tulisa countered. The red mist descended and Gerasimou hurled abuse at Tulisa. He called her a 'scumbag trying to replace Cheryl'. When he moved towards the front of the stage she told him, 'Stand back – don't invade my space.' He then told her to shut up and added an insult that was censored by the programme but which provoked looks of horror. Tulisa told him he had embarrassed himself 'in front of the entire nation'. As he was led from the stage by security, she told him, 'I've worked my way up from Camden Town,' and thumping the desk to emphasise her point, added: 'That's why I'm here today.' The cheer of support from the audience was far louder than the edited programme suggested. Many audience members rose to their feet in support of Tulisa.

Backstage, Gerasimou's foul-mouthed rant continued.

Pointing at Tulisa on the backstage monitors he said, 'No dogs allowed – I didn't know dogs were allowed on *The X Factor* or I'd have bought my f**king Alsatian!' This enraged Dermot O'Leary who pointed menacingly at him and said, 'George – watch your mouth.' It was no bad thing for Tulisa's popularity for her to be shown under attack so early in the series. Nothing rallies *X Factor* viewers more quickly than an act that appears far too big for their boots. In the case of Gerasimou, his attack on Tulisa was portrayed as so utterly petulant and unfounded that she was undoubtedly the sympathetic figure in the battle of words. The fact she so pluckily defended herself and her presence on the show only added to the glory of the moment.

Gerasimou was later interviewed online about the confrontation. He said, 'I actually rated Tulisa before that but when I went on *X Factor* I got to know what she was really like. Honestly, I wouldn't urinate on her if she burst into flames.' He went on to blame Tulisa for the spat, saying she was 'out to make me lose my temper', and conceded that he 'came out of it as a clown'. Asked what insult he had thrown at her in the segment that was censored on the broadcast, he said he called Tulisa a 'Camden whore'. He rounded off his rather sour interview by calling Tulisa a 'cheap Cheryl', Rowland a 'cheap Beyoncé' and Barlow 'a cheap Cowell'. It was clear that time had not mellowed him. The drama only added to the appeal of the opening episode. From the perspective of Tulisa's popularity it gave viewers the chance to rally behind her as she faced off a foul-mouthed bore. As she would have been all too aware, this was helpful for her. After the show was broadcast, she received a text message from Simon Cowell. It was his verdict she cared about more than anyone's. 'He said he was completely happy and there were no notes for improvements,' she said. 'So I guess I passed!'

The viewers had also been impressed, though those of them who had been aware of Tulisa prior to the series noticed she seemed thinner on the show. She later dismissed theories that arose that she had gone on a crash diet. 'The only time I lost weight was two years ago after I saw myself in a bikini,' she told *Now* magazine. 'I didn't mind because I was still toned, but I realised I'm more comfortable being the weight I've always been. I don't know how it happened, but it just slipped off. I've never tried to lose weight. I'm always 8-8 ½st – that's where I am now. The biggest I've been is 9st.' Still, so far so good. In a future episode Tulisa's emotions would soar to the surface. Indeed, a spectacular outburst was just around the corner for the newcomer.

'The last thing I thought was that I'd be crying on national TV,' she told the *Mirror* about the audition in question. 'It happened early in the auditions and it wasn't just a Cheryl tear. We're talking floodgates. I couldn't stop. This one person performed and all the emotions built up. It was overwhelming – they really got me, then there was the realisation I was actually doing *The X Factor*, that my life had changed, and it all came out.' Michelle Barrett had sung 'All The Man I Need' by Whitney Houston, after telling the judges of the sacrifices she had made in life to look after her children. Her devotion to her maternal duties had, she said, prevented her from making it as a singer. It was a pleasant rendition and when it came to the comments from the judges, Tulisa was the first to speak. 'You remind me of my mum,' she said, clearly trying to hold back tears. 'It was brilliant. Just like you, Mum had a beautiful voice and she didn't do anything with it.' The she compared the sacrifices both Barrett, and her mother had made for their children. She drew on memories of her own mother 'standing in the kitchen' and singing with her amazing voice. The contestant became so overwhelmed that she too started crying. Tulisa said to her fellow judges, 'You guys are going to think I'm nuts, but this is a mummy and daughter thing going on.'

After the audition, Tulisa explained further to Barlow, Rowland and Walsh why she had felt so emotional. 'Me and my mum have got this really powerful relationship, she's the reason that I sing,' she told them. 'She had the most powerful voice and never did anything with it –she had me, she became unwell and then, you know, she spent her life still singing in the kitchen, and I wish she'd got up and done that because she has a voice just like that. Amazing. I can't believe I just got that emotional.' She added that her friends teased her about how unemotional a person she is. 'They say that getting emotion out of you is like drawing blood from a stone, but you bring my mum into it and that's it!'

On the evening that this edition was broadcast, Tulisa's mother seems to have got the wrong end of the stick and thought the drama was being broadcast live. According to Tulisa, she received a phone call from Ann: she seemed to believe that the audition she had just watched on ITV had taken place the same evening. Tulisa was very amused by the misunderstanding and reassured Ann that the audition – and her upset – had taken place several months previously. She then put the phone down and shared the humorous mix-up with her Twitter followers. 'As if my mum called me 2nit going "r u ok love? stop crying!"...ITS NOT LIVE YET MUM! I'm sitting eating my dinner! Haha she cracks me up.'

It was a light-hearted and amusing conclusion to an emotional moment in the series. And so to boot camp, which began on a dramatic and controversial note. Having gathered 186 acts for the boot camp round, the judges immediately axed 40 of them before a single note had been sung. It certainly made for sensational viewing, but many viewers felt enormous sympathy for the 40 acts who had had their hopes raised by being told they were 'through to boot camp' and who had travelled from across the country to be there, only to be sent home as part of a premeditated twist. It seemed cruel.

With boot camp completed, each judge discovered which of the categories they had been chosen to mentor. Traditionally, the judges are keen to avoid the groups category but for Tulisa the opposite was true. 'The category that I need in my life is the groups,' she said.

(Barlow, on the other hand, declared: 'If I get the groups...I'm leaving' and Walsh said: 'As long as I don't get the groups, I don't care.') As Tulisa approached the door behind which her category had been assembled, she said: 'I feel unprofessional now because I'm so emotional.' She so wanted the groups and when she saw she did indeed have them, she leapt up and down on the spot with sheer joy. 'Guys, you can't even imagine how emotional I'm feeling right now,' she told them. 'From now on, I am here 100 per cent for all of you. From the bottom of my heart.' She then told them they were going to Greece for the judges' houses phase.

Outside, she told O'Leary, 'I now want to be the first *X Factor* judge to take the groups to the finals and win the competition. Here comes the competition – now I'm ready, now I'm ready, baby!' Confident, almost defiant words, but how well placed her confidence turned out to be. At the time, though, few people shared her confidence. The bands category did seem very weak at first. Even ex-Oasis guitarist Noel Gallagher, an unlikely fan of the show and a man who had been personally approached by Simon Cowell to be a judge on this very series of the show, was moved to discuss this. His prognosis was not encouraging for the bands category. 'I watched this series for the first time this weekend,' he told *Digital Spy* in October. 'I'm usually quite good at picking who is going to go through, and I think I managed to pick them all correctly this time. The groups are f**king appalling; they really are f**king dreadful!'

There would clearly need to be some surgery performed to save the band category. Fortunately, Tulisa had a crafty plan. First, though, she had some more simple decisions to make. She put through 2 Shoes – a pair of Essex girls, Nu Vibe – a boy band, and Rhythmix, a girl band put together from girls who had originally auditioned as solo artists. As is custom, the drama of each decision was played out for all it could be as each act stood in agony, waiting for the decision to be announced. She told 2 Shoes she admired their combination of a fun, novelty act with genuine vocal talent, but then said she was not sure there was a big enough market for them. Having given them mixed hints, she said: 'Girls – I'm taking you through to the live shows!' Teasingly, she told Nu Vibe, 'Guys, I am so sorry...but...you're going to have to put up with me a lot longer.' They raced towards her, and judge and act celebrated in a huddle like a football team. She used the same trick with Rhythmix, who she told: 'I'm very sorry...but you're going to have to do this all over again.'

Then came her masterstroke to strengthen the category. After sending home two bands, The Risk and Chasing Keys, she created a 'supergroup' by combining Chasing Keys' Charlie Healy with Andrew Merry, Derry Mensah and Ashley J Baptiste – three fifths of The Risk. She kept the latter band name for the supergroup, which would hitherto be called The Risk. She told them: 'I liked both of the groups. But I didn't believe either of them were potential winners. You four stood out for me within your groups, so I've decided to offer you the chance to be my supergroup. I am going to keep you guys as The Risk – you're my risk, and I believe in you.'

It was a bold move – and one that received inevitable criticism from some. The raciest of the angles of objection was the perception that she had sent home the majority of the band Chasing Keys because she felt they were too posh. With three members of the band having attended a public school in Hertfordshire, the accusation made was that Tulisa had found them unconvincing as rappers. She never commented specifically on that, but she later admitted that the move was 'controversial' and said she expected more of a backlash for it than she received. 'I came up with the idea. I knew when it came to those two boy bands it had to be one or the other. And then the night before, it was about one in the morning, I turned around and asked the producer if I could do it. And he said, "Are you ready for it? Do you really want to do it?" and I said, "Yes, I'm ready."'

She was also ready for the live shows.

CHAPTER EIGHT

With the live shows around the corner, Tulisa realised that not only was she now utterly absorbed in the series and its multiple machinations, but that she would be for some months ahead. As many who have been involved in *The X Factor* have found, it is an all-encompassing experience that one either embraces in full or has to leave alone. Although she knew that when she signed up, the magnitude of it only dawned on her once she was firmly involved. 'I'm just living it and breathing it at the moment and I'm spending a lot of time with the contestants. I was with them last night and I get very emotionally attached to them as well. I was at the house all day long, cooking them dinner, asking, "Have you eaten?", "Are you alright?" ... and yeah, it becomes your life.' From the mother hen of N-Dubz to the mother hen of *The X Factor*, Tulisa was proving quite the clucky character.

During the live shows, the media obsession with the series becomes nothing short of monstrous. It was perhaps for this reason that as the series progressed, Tulisa and Fazer had finally begun to go public about their relationship. Having been together since 2010, they had kept it quiet for some time. It was Fazer who confirmed the rumours when he said: "I've got a glow about me, I'm in love. She's the one. I'm in love with a great girl.' Of her *X Factor* challenge to come, he could not have been more supportive in his words. 'She's got a special aura about her. I just think she stands out and she has a real opinion. I don't think words can describe how proud I am of her. We're going to support her for the live shows definitely.' Tulisa added: 'He's my rock – he's been there for me throughout the past few months. I couldn't be doing what I'm doing without him,' the star revealed.

She would need strength aplenty during the live finals. The opening show saw each judge, in an *X Factor* first, forced to drop one of their four acts. There was no public vote. It was an excruciating moment for each judge, Tulisa said she suffered so much that she 'cried tears' over it. The band she sent home was 2 Shoes. After she delivered the decision, a tearful Tulisa told them: 'I can't even find a reason to say why... I had to pick one act, and I'm so sorry, girls.' She added: 'I class you as my friends now and I swear, I swear I want to stay in touch with you.' She then embraced them. Of all the judges, she had seemed to take this part of the process hardest. If she thought that had been a difficult week, she had a far tougher one just around the corner.

In week two, she lost her act Nu Vibe. The bottom two had been her band and Frankie Cocozza. Barlow, unsurprisingly, voted to protect his own act Cocozza by sending home Nu Vibe. Rowland then also voted against the band. O'Leary then asked Tulisa for her decision. 'I think it's pretty obvious, Dermot,' she said. 'It's a shame you guys are here tonight. Honestly, the act I'm sending home is Frankie.' So it came down to Louis Walsh. He said that both acts had had a bad night the previous evening. 'The act I'm going to have to send home is – Nu Vibe,' he said. Tulisa had lost her first act during the public vote shows. Asked by O'Leary what had gone wrong, she said: 'I'm not sure – all I can say is I believed in them, I took a chance, they worked hard, they gave everything.' She said she still believed in them, but 'it happens.' The following week there would be real trouble for her, as a row erupted that would cast a shadow over her for the rest of the series.

In week three, the live show was given a stunning climax when Misha B took to the stage last. She sang the Prince song 'Purple Rain' and had the audience in raptures with her powerful and soulful rendition. Such a performance would normally have merited a clean sweep of praise from the judging panel. However, there was a hint that trouble was brewing right from the off, when Louis Walsh delivered his verdict. At first he praised Misha's performance, but concluded his verdict saying: 'You're very confident, you're a very confident performer. I hope you're not too overconfident.' It was then Tulisa's turn to speak. Like Walsh, she began with some positive comments about

Misha's performance on the night and talent in general. She, too, followed this praise with some remarks that called into question Misha's character. 'There is no doubt about it, when it comes to talent you are way up there,' she told Misha. 'Most people, they come into the competition and they need to be built up and progress but you came as a whole package and you are definitely the star of the show. But I do have one negative this week. I think you are very competitive and I've seen a different side of you backstage and you don't realise that you do it, but in some ways you being so feisty can come across as quite mean to certain contestants and I've been told by a few this week there's been a few mean comments towards them.'

As eyebrows were raised and a few boos rang out, Tulisa added: 'I'm not putting you down but take that feistiness and energy when you get on the stage and leave them all behind. Put aside the attitude.' Barlow then insisted that what happened backstage should not be mentioned on air. 'I don't care what goes on backstage and we shouldn't be getting involved in that,' he said. 'I mentioned earlier we were looking for an artist that can sell albums and there she is right there. Amazing vocals, great vision, well done Misha.' Rowland added her own comments, launching a defence of Misha. She then turned to Walsh, and suggested that some of his acts could do with more confidence. Walsh then turned up the heat by adding: 'One of my contestants has complained about Misha bullying her backstage.'

The use of the word 'bullying' gave the issue an incendiary dimension and the show a fiery conclusion. The producers had hoped for more excitement and controversy to help boost ratings. To what extent the airing of this controversy had been pre-planned was unclear, but whether pre-meditated or not, this row had given the series some edge. In the spin-off *Xtra Factor* show, which followed the main broadcast, this issue was the source of discussion. Again, Tulisa came under fire for what she had said. She defended herself, saying that if someone had made a 'bitchy comment' to one of her acts backstage then she had a right to raise it. 'I feel like if you are going to portray a certain person on stage, it should be the same person that's backstage,' she added.

Later, Misha was asked for her response to Tulisa and Walsh's allegations. She admitted that things had got 'heated' backstage, but added: 'Tulisa hurt my feelings because there are two sides to every story.' The controversy became the source of feverish discussion among viewers on Twitter. Ironically, even though Walsh had made the most specific and grave allegation against Misha, it was Tulisa who was being cast as the being the main critic of Misha. Celebrity 'Tweeters' got involved, with even tennis player Boris Becker weighing in with: 'Misha B is by far the best !!! Don't understand judge Tulisa at all !!!'

Over the following 24 hours, as the public voted ahead of the Sunday evening results show, the story raged on. *X Factor* 'sources' claimed that Rowland had 'screamed' at producers backstage, venting her fury that they had allowed Tulisa to 'get away with something like that'. 'Friends' of Rowland claimed she had said of her relationship with Tulisa, 'It's war!' During the Sunday show, Walsh apologised for part of his criticism of Misha. 'I shouldn't have called Misha a bully and I apologise for that,' he said. Fears that Misha might have suffered in the voting as a result of Tulisa and Walsh's remarks were put aside when she was announced as through to the next week. It was Sami Brookes – Walsh'who left the show after finishing in the bottom two.

The following day, Sami denied that there had been any bullying, saying such an idea was 'laughable and ridiculous'. Misha admitted to the *Mirror* that she had been a playground bully at school but had since changed. Meanwhile, Tulisa was mostly focused on a positive – that both her acts had finished outside the dreaded bottom two after the public vote. She took her remaining groups, The Risk and Rhythmix, for a celebratory night out at Whisky Mist in Mayfair, London. Tulisa had changed out of the metallic green dress she had worn on stage, and opted for a black strapless tiered dress. She looked sensational: both relaxed and stylish. Once more this focused attention on just how much time she was spending with her acts. As questions were raised over how much time Rowland and Walsh were spending mentoring their acts, Tulisa was again seen to be both working and playing hard with hers.

With the media keen to paint tensions between Tulisa and Rowland, particular attention was paid to the amount of time that Tulisa spent with Rowland's act Sophie Habibis. They spent a long time chatting and were also photographed holding hands. With Rowland having flown to America, Tulisa and Habibis were bonding over their shared north London experiences and Mediterranean roots. However, Tulisa had reportedly been furious when Rowland had offered advice to one of her acts, Rhythmix. There would be a twist in the tale of Tulisa's friendship with Habibis at the next live results show.

At least Tulisa could smile at the praise she was receiving from Andrew Merry, a member of her band The Risk. Merry spoke warmly of the attention she paid to her acts. This went as far, he said, as her cooking them dinner. 'She's got some serious skills,' he said. 'She's amazing.' Of her more direct mentoring skills, he said: 'Obviously we speak to her on a regular basis. She looks after us if we've got any problems, she'll come and help us out. Obviously she's the boss, so you've got to make sure you're working hard and she'll look after you.' So there was no shortage of respect and gratitude to Tulisa from Merry. Indeed, his feelings even went as far as the romantic. Admitting to something of a crush on his mentor, he said: 'I'm just buzzing whenever I say her name.'

For Tulisa, this was music to her ears. Indeed, she was relieved by the public's attitude towards The Risk. As well as voting them through two weeks running, the public had not responded as fiercely to her forming a 'supergroup' out of two other acts as she had feared. With her know-how of the machinations of the music industry, this manipulation by her was nothing out of the ordinary. As she said, things like this took place behind the scenes all the time at record labels and pop management firms. Indeed, bands such as

The Spice Girls and Westlife went under personnel changes before the final, winning formula had been struck upon. She had expected this to cause more of a stir among the public. 'It was controversial,' she said. 'And I'm not going to lie, I expected a bigger backlash than what I got. I know people take this very seriously and I panicked a little bit – but I said I can't put through one of these groups if I don't believe that they can win.'

As the week wore on, Tulisa found her every move being interpreted through the prism of the supposed row with Rowland. She added fuel to the fiery speculation by sending out some cryptic messages on Twitter. One of them read: 'So many Conspiracies in this world, we all need 2 open r minds, including myself.....we learn something everyday'. As her followers wondered whether that was in reference to the goings-on between herself and Rowland, she sent another cryptic message that read simply: 'Omg tots awks...' Another message mentioned 'Emotional drama'. Between them, these Tweets certainly increased the intrigue around the show.

This controversy certainly suited the needs of the *X Factor* producers, who had been put under pressure to increase ratings. The increased attention on Tulisa came as she prepared to launch her own perfume. Called The Female Boss, its slightly cheesy official description claimed: it had 'top notes of subtle spices, gentle rose and sweet jasmine to create a feminine floral heart. It's not overpowering, but quietly confident, like Tulisa herself.' The packaging was, interestingly, much more redolent of

Tulisa's N-Dubz years than her new *X Factor* image. The box featured a photograph of Tulisa taken before her *X Factor* makeover, and the lettering on the box and bottle were both in a graffiti, N-Dubz font.

At the press launch for the perfume, at The Perfume Shop in London's Oxford Street, Tulisa wore a distinctive black dress with red stripes criss-crossing and white squares. In colour scheme and design it was similar to the famous *X Factor* logo. However, if coordination had been intended it could just have easily been to tie in with The Perfume Shop logo, which featured the same colours and a similar design. The dress was said to have been designed by Karen Millen. One bitchy press report on the launch suggested that her outfit's similarity to the shop's logo made her appear like she was a girl employed by the store. However, with black heels and her hair in a semi-bouffant, she looked stylish and stunning as the press snapped away at her.

It is difficult to launch a celebrity perfume with statements that are anything other than a bit fatuous, as many other celebrity scent-launchers have found. Tulisa told the assembled press that she 'wanted a fragrance that I could relate to'. She added that her design was to create:'something powerful without losing its girlieness. I wanted to be able to wear it day and night. This fragrance will really give the girls the confidence to show those boys who is boss.' Cheesy stuff, but no more so than the statements uttered by other celebrities who have launched their own scents. At the Oxford Street launch, hundreds of

Tulisa's fans queued for several hours to be able to meet her at the event. She announced during it that she had plans to launch a clothing line. Mindful of the age and background of many of her admirers, she said: 'Lots of my fans are young girls so I want to make sure they don't have to spend a lot of money.' Speaking of her own wider plans, she added: 'Then I want to expand into other areas. I'd love to be known as a successful female businesswoman worldwide.' Fazer had, in 2010, also said he wished to launch his own clothing line. For it he envisaged a name: Na Na Wear. Imaginative, or perhaps not.

* * * *

Back in *X Factor* land, she was at the heart of the story again. Almost lost amid the ongoing controversy over Tulisa and Walsh's remarks about Misha were Tulisa's comments about the performance of Frankie Cocozza, which had been criticial. 'I really enjoyed myself on stage,' he said. 'I wasn't too impressed with my comments, but I can't do anything about that. Tulisa said that I'd lost my innocence, but I don't think I've ever been innocent if I'm honest.' He snapped that any criticisms he received from Tulisa and the rest of the panel only fuelled his determination. 'Hearing the bad comments from the judges makes you determined and makes you want to do better.'

Next, Tulisa had more work to do when a member of her band The Risk dropped a bombshell on her. Ashley J Baptiste threw an almighty spanner in the works when he told Tulisa: 'This isn't for me. It's the hardest thing I've ever done.' She was shocked, but soon adapted to the news philosophically. 'He had to do what was right for him,' she reasoned. She had to decide what to do in the wake of this news – and fast. Unlike the everyday pop world, where a band's commitments could be put on hold while a new member was carefully chosen, the weekly demands of *The X Factor* dictated a swift resolution. Using the same creativity and daring that she had employed to put together The Risk in the first place, Tulisa decided to refer back to Nu Vibe. She thought that band's member Ashford Campbell would be a neat replacement for Baptiste. She asked both parties if they were happy with her plan and checked with producers that it would be permitted. Having got the green light, she made her decision official: Campbell would join The Risk immediately. The three remaining original members of The Risk issued a statement giving the thumbs-up to Tulisa's move. 'He's mega talented and will bring so many qualities to group,' they said. 'We're so glad he said yes and we can't wait to get rehearsing.'

Meanwhile, an eventful week for Tulisa was capped when her band Rhythmix was forced to change its name. A youth charity based in Brighton was dismayed when it learned that its name was also being used by the band. It said its work with tens of thousands of young people over the past 12 years was being put 'at risk' by the band's name. A Facebook campaign was launched by the charity, demanding that the band change its name. This came to a head, in the week after the Misha controversy, when

Tulisa's band announced it would change its name to Little Mix. Even then the charity was not entirely satisfied. Its chief executive complained that it had taken too long for the matter to be resolved. He even called for *X Factor* bosses to pay the legal costs the charity had incurred after hiring lawyers.

At the live show on Saturday, the personnel change in The Risk was eclipsed by another swap: on the judges' panel. Kelly Rowland was reportedly too ill to fly home from America for the weekend's shows. It was announced that 2008 *X Factor* winner Alexandra Burke would sit in for Rowland on the weekend's shows. Burke's presence brought a fresh energy to the show, quite literally in the form of the excited delivery of her verdicts. At one stage she reacted angrily to some comments from Walsh, and concluded her outburst 'OK dot com,' much to the side-split amusement of many viewers on Twitter. The Burke verdict that most impacted on Tulisa was not for one of the bands, but for Habibis, of whom Tulisa had grown so fond. Although Burke was ostensibly replacing Rowland, that did not mean she gave automatic positive feedback to the American singer's acts. When it came to Habibis, Burke followed damning verdicts from Walsh and Barlow with a not entirely complimentary judgement herself. Her positives about Habibis were lukewarm, and she added that there had been a 'slight tuning problem' with her rendition of 'Bang Bang (My Baby Shot Me Down)'.

On the following evening's results show, Tulisa was delighted when her remaining acts The Risk and Little Mix were both safely voted through. Indeed, for many viewers and commentators Little Mix had been the pick of the bunch in the previous evening's live show. Their striking take on the Katy Perry song 'ET' had united the panel and most viewers. Tulisa felt great as she left the stage, with both her acts intact after the dreaded public vote. However, as she took her seat back on the panel, her joy was tempered by the realisation that the bottom two would be Misha B and Habibis. For Tulisa it was difficult to decide which of the pair to vote to save. On the one hand, she admired the talent of Habibis and had also grown very close to the young Londoner. However, she admired the rich talent of Misha, whose style of music came closer to that of N-Dubz than any of the other contestants. Furthermore, Tulisa was keenly aware that the public would view her decision through the prism of the previous weekend's controversy between her and Misha. If she saved Habibis, she realised, a lot of people would see this as her sticking a second knife into Misha. Decisions, decisions!

Walsh had, predictably, already voted to save Misha B when it came to Tulisa's turn to speak. She announced that she and Misha had addressed their issues from the previous weekend, and added that she would have to base her decision on music, rather than 'personalities and connections'. Already, things were looking bleak for Habibis. 'I have to go to the person I can most relate to musically, the person who represents the music from my roots,' added Tulisa, before announcing she would send Habibis home. After Rowland came to the same decision –

via a telephone link-up – Misha B was saved and Habibis left the competition.

It had been a tough moment for Tulisa to send Habibis home. Their bond and friendship had been strong from when they first met during the competition. Tulisa would have loved to save her friend, but she had told herself from the moment she first signed the contract to be an *X Factor* judge that she would approach everything during the show with the utmost honesty and integrity. Though it had been a tough week for her, it ended with her standing tall. Not only had she successfully negotiated her two acts through the public vote, she had also seen Little Mix soar in popularity and respect. The crowning high for Tulisa came when the public saw her put aside a personal friendship with Habibis to vote honestly. What an eventful seven days it had been – and Tulisa had been the only *X Factor* judge to get into the Halloween spirit by wearing a cat-woman outfit for the Saturday evening show, complete with pointy ears.

The weekend's drama had done little to dispel perceptions that Tulisa and Rowland had genuinely fallen out. Barlow insisted that all the drama on the panel was genuine and that relations between judges did get 'heated'. He went on to single out Tulisa for praise. '[She] is brilliant,' he said. 'To come onto the panel as a complete beginner and put those groups together like she did, shows a real eye for talent. I hope one of her groups gets through to the final few. They're very lucky to have her – she spends a lot of time and energy on them.'

Another of Barlow's comments in this interview with *Heat* magazine was a critical one of Walsh, who he accused of spending insufficient time with his acts. Meanwhile, another newspaper placed Walsh and Tulisa in the centre of an alleged fresh controversy. It was claimed that Cowell, tired of the slipping viewing figures for the show, had charged Walsh with the responsibility of shaking up the judges' panel. The chief option being mulled over by Walsh was, reportedly, replacing Tulisa with former *X Factor* judge Cheryl Cole. It was safe to say that no such swap was ever in danger of happening, and that this story could be filed under the 'hype' category. Meanwhile, Rowland arrived back in Britain after her prolonged absence. She looked in decent health as she arrived at LAX Airport for the flight to the UK. With a dash of irony, no sooner had Rowland recovered than Tulisa fell ill. She pulled out of all promotional arrangements for her perfume after being hit by toothache.

In another, ultimately successful, bid to boost ratings, the show's producers decided to stage a double elimination the following weekend. As the public debated which two acts would leave the competition, few predicted that either of Tulisa's remaining acts would be in danger of the dreaded chop. Both Little Mix and The Risk were, in fact, most often discussed as potential finalists or even as becoming the first band to win *The X Factor*. So what a shock it was when The Risk finished bottom in that weekend's public vote, thus becoming the first act to leave on the night. It had been an entertaining weekend of

X Factor. On the Saturday evening the acts sang 'club classics' songs. From Johnny Robinson's camp opener to Little Mix's superb rendition of 'Don't Stop The Music' at the top of the show, it was an entertaining evening. The performance generally regarded as the low-point of the show was Frankie Cocozza's chaotic take on 'I Gotta Feeling' by Black Eyed Peas. Given that he had already been considered likely to be voted out, lots of viewers expected that the bottom two would be Cocozza plus one other. Robinson was tipped to join him, in part because he had performed in the opening slot, known as the 'graveyard slot' due to the fact that the opener act is often forgotten by the time the voting lines open at the end of the show.

On the following evening's results show there was widespread shock when O'Leary announced the results of the public vote, and it was revealed that Cocozza had survived a place in the bottom three. As gasps rang across the audience, even Cocozza seemed shocked and a little embarrassed to have survived. The shock became deeper when it sunk in that The Risk was in the bottom three alongside Robinson and the controversial Kitty Brucknell. Tulisa looked devastated. All she could hope for now was that they had not finished bottom, as that act would be sent home immediately, leaving the other two to battle for survival in the 'sing-off'. However, Tulisa's act was not going to be permitted any such lifeline. To her surprise and horror, it quickly transpired they *had* finished bottom of the public vote and would be eliminated immediately. The stunned expression on Tulisa's face said it all. Meanwhile, O'Leary asked the band why they thought they had finished bottom. Risk member Derry Mensah replied: 'I don't know what it is, I'm just happy that we're here together.' The band's de facto front man Charlie Healy confirmed that the band planned to 'carry on' together, while Andrew Merry added: 'It's been an absolute honour to sing with these guys, it's been an amazing experience. Thanks to everyone who's helped us along the way.' Then it was time to wave them goodbye. After the sing-off Robinson was sent home by the judges, allowing Brucknell to survive another week.

Afterwards, Tulisa was asked what she thought had caused her previously fancied band to crash out of the voting public's favour. 'I don't know,' she said, still clearly shaken and upset. 'I think maybe the band changeover, the dramas affected them probably… I don't know.' Whenshe was asked whether her initial manufacturing of the band and the subsequent line-up change prior to the previous weekend's show had played a part, Tulisa attempted an answer but it was clear she was still in a state of some disbelief as she addressed that theory. 'Yeah there's a possibility, maybe that's why they were getting so much support until now but honestly I have no idea,' she continued. 'It was honestly a massive shock for me tonight, I'm not denying that. I'm totally baffled. I don't think they deserved to go at all.' Despite admitting that her line-up changes and manufacturing of the band might have been responsible for their exit, Tulisa was absolutely clear that she had no regrets over her actions. It is not in Tulisa's nature to back down easily on a decision she has made. She was not about to do so here. 'I definitely do not regret one moment of creating those groups or watching them perform or watching them grow or getting to know them,' she said. 'For me it's been a good experience for me and for them and life-changing for them because they're going to go on to do good things and I can never regret changing someone's life, no way.'

Tulisa had to pick herself up and begin another week of working on keeping her one remaining act in the running. Little Mix was growing in stature each week and Tulisa was determined for so many reasons to give them her backing. Firstly, they were her act, secondly they were her only remaining act and thirdly, she felt a sense of sisterhood with the girls and was keen to buck the *X Factor* trend of girl bands being unsuccessful. Tulisa had carefully, and not entirely inaccurately, positioned them as everyday girls who female voters should relate to, rather than envy. All the same, the band and their mentor faced a huge mental obstacle. In fact, Tulisa had a double trend to buck. No band had ever won *The X Factor*. The closest were G4 and JLS who had finished runners-up to Steve Brookstein and Alexandra Burke respectively. If Tulisa could take Little Mix all the way, she would be making *X Factor* history, as well as being the winning mentor. Quite a target to aim for.

As she continued to adjust to the tensions and pressures of the live shows, particularly the perceived rivalry with

Rowland, Tulisa reportedly asked her predecessor Cheryl Cole for advice. An unnamed 'source' reportedly told the *Sunday Mirror*: 'The row with Kelly really got to her [Tulisa] and she has been on good terms with Cheryl for a while so she sent her some messages to see if she could help.' The 'source' added: 'Cheryl has been through it all and told her to just enjoy herself and try to patch things up with Kelly. Tulisa feels much better, thanks to Cheryl.' The veracity of this unattributed story was increased when Cole herself spoke about Tulisa days later. In the first interview from Cole since she had been controversially removed from the judging panel for *The X Factor USA*, she spoke of her liking for Tulisa. 'She's lovely, I've known her for years,' Cheryl told *InStyle* magazine in the much-hyped interview. 'She came to my birthday party.' Cole then scoffed at the perceptions that she had a grudge against Tulisa or that she would not be watching the UK *X Factor*. 'You know what's funny? People are surprised I say I'll be watching and that I'm a fan of Tulisa's, but all they know is what they read in the gossip magazines and it tends to be crap.'

Back at *X Factor* HQ, the official story was that Tulisa and Rowland had made up. Tulisa said, 'We're cool' but she was not in an entirely placatory mood. 'All this stuff about me not speaking to Kelly is not true,' she said, but added: 'She wasn't speaking to *me*.' She also confirmed the suspicions that the advice Rowland gave her on how to mentor her bands had also caused tension to rise between them. 'Yeah, she was giving me tips on things, like showing me clothes she thought might work for Little Mix,' she said. 'But it's not like I'm gonna ignore something that's a good idea. I just didn't like it at the time. I didn't go mad. We just disagreed.' More interesting was Tulisa's revelation that she and Rowland had had a conversation about not just the show and the music industry, but also about life in general. It had been a healthy exchange between the two female judges, who found that they had more uniting them than dividing them. 'We had a long chat on Saturday night – a proper chat about the show and personal stuff too. It's quite stressful being on the show and there's so much going on I don't think we ever had time to just talk about everything.' She added: 'We actually have a lot in common, which might surprise some people. We might even do a collaboration when I do my solo stuff. There you go, bet you didn't think I'd say that?' She also said she hoped the public would realise that it was passion and not petulance that fuelled her behaviour in the competition. She was not, she insisted, being 'stroppy'.

Meanwhile, she was also focused on life beyond *The X Factor*. Participation in the show can become so overwhelming and all-encompassing that those involved can easily forget that life continues beyond the bubble of the show. Tulisa, though, was looking to the future and her plans to launch herself as both a solo music artist and also a celebrity in her own right, beyond the connections with *The X Factor* and N-Dubz. 'My plan is to release my first single in February and then put out two or three before my album comes out,' she said. 'N-Dubz are having a break.

We might not do anything for up to two years. We're putting out a greatest hits record on November 28 which I hope the fans – new and old – will love. We put our heart and soul into our music so it's kind of a celebration of the best stuff we've done.'

Another plan she had was to publish a novel. Addressing suspicions that 'celebrity' authors are sometimes not the author of the novels they publish but simply sign off a manuscript entirely created by someone else, Tulisa insisted this was her novel. She said she was busy working on storyboards for the book, which would chart the life of a Tulisa-esque woman. She hoped that 2012 would be the year that she truly launched herself as a personality in her own right. What would the younger Tulisa who, even before N-Dubz achieved fame, had happily admitted that she wanted to be famous, make of her plans and stature? She would have loved it. More recently, in 2010, she had said: 'In 10 years time I want to be right at the top. Simple as.' She spoke of her lust to achieve international fame, including popularity in America. That will be a big ask, but Tulisa certainly seems to possess the ambition, determination and strength of character to give it the very best crack she can.

Meanwhile, her next big ambition was to take Little Mix all the way in *The X Factor*.

CHAPTER
NINE

As *The X Factor* live shows carried on, it was time to assess how successful Tulisa had been as a judge. The London newspaper *Metro* did just that in a kind of 'half-term report' feature. The article described her as 'an unusual appointment to *The X Factor* panel and [the one with] the most to prove'. The article said that to her credit her presence on the show drew in 'the youth quotient', but said she was 'ill-equipped to mentor groups when her only band experience is performing with a man in a chullo hat that raps about Facebook'. Most viewers, however, were giving increasingly positive feedback about her performances. With Cowell, too, in admiration of her and with her act Little Mix improving each week, Tulisa could afford to be confident about her *X Factor* time to date.

However, assessments of the judging panel were upstaged by the ongoing saga of the season's most controversial contestant – Frankie Cocozza. His abrupt departure from the competition handed one of Tulisa's acts a potential lifeline. Ever since his first audition, in which he said he was entering the competition to boost his chances with girls and then bared his buttocks, upon which he had tattooed names of girls he had slept with, Cocozza had divided opinion. His fans admired his rebellious nature, wild appearance and the hedonistic lifestyle that was so hyped by the press. His detractors thought him an untalented, ungracious act, ill deserving of his place in the live finals. After several weeks of live shows, during one of which Cocozza worsened his standing by celebrating his progression with an aggressively shouted swear word, many in the public were puzzled as to why he remained in the competition. Even his own mentor Barlow had at times been nothing short of damning of his act's performances. Suddenly, midweek between two shows, it was announced he had left the show. This came after he was caught 'breaking competition rules', according to the show's producers.

Speculation as to what his rule-breaking had consisted of was rife. There were widespread utterances of 'good riddance' as Cocozza disappeared into the sunset. One of Tulisa's acts spoke in his support. 'He's all right really,' said Andrew Merry of The Risk. 'If you see him behind the scenes he's a good laugh. I just wish the public could see what we see because he's such a good laugh and a likeable character.' (Cocozza has since tried to resurrect his career, including an appearance in *Celebrity Big Brother*.) Tulisa and a number of *X Factor* viewers hoped that Cocozza's exit would see The Risk reinstated to the competition. Others expressed the opinion that the fairest move would be to bring the most recently eliminated act – Johnny Robinson – back into the fold.

Neither move would transpire. One of Tulisa's acts would be given the chance to return, but not The Risk. Instead, it would be 2 Shoes who were handed the potential lifeline. In one of the more perplexing manipulations in *X Factor* history, producers announced that one of 2 Shoes, James Michael, Amelia Lily or Jonjo Kerr – who were all eliminated in the first week of the live shows – would fill the gap left by Cocozza. The confusion over this move quickly gave way to speculation. Was this move designed purely to get the popular Amelia Lily, removed from the competition by her mentor Rowland before the public had had a chance to give its verdict on her via the voting lines? As such, was this a thinly veiled slap-down of Rowland from the show's producers? Other theories included suggestions that the entire plot had been written in advance, with Cocozza always destined for an early exit, allowing an always waiting-in-the-wings Lily to return and storm to victory.

And all this before the public had even voted which of the four eliminated acts they would choose to bring back. At least it took the heat off Tulisa. Though she realised that of the four eliminated acts, hers was the least likely to be reinstated by the public, she also realised that among all the attention being paid to Cocozza and Lily some was critical of two of her rival judges. Barlow's judgement in putting Cocozza through to the live shows raised question marks against his judgement, as did Rowland's decision to remove Lily from the first week of the live shows. With Walsh also facing repeated suggestions from the viewers that he had gone stale having been on the show since its inception, it was Tulisa who in many ways was retaining most dignity and respect as a judge and mentor. No journalistic assessments of her performance on the show could conceal that.

Meanwhile, Tulisa had some fresh campaigning to do. As competitive and focused as ever, she was keen to drum up support for a return by her act, 2 Shoes. The phone lines for viewers to vote on which of the four acts to return opened on the Friday before the next live show, during which they would close again and a count would be taken. The favourite to return remained Lily, but Tulisa was not about to take that as read. Indeed, she campaigned cleverly for 2 Shoes. Mindful that there was a constituency that had been sad to see the fun Johnny Robinson leave, she appealed to that constituency while encouraging votes for 2 Shoes. She said: 'Now Johnny [Robinson]'s gone the big fun factor is missing and the truth is I never wanted to get rid of my girls in the first place. I just had to make a decision and unfortunately those guys left and they never got to show us what they can really do.' She went on: 'I think they can bring something different to the show and I think that it needs it right now considering the mood, so they definitely can come back and spice things up.'

As it turned out, the Saturday night show saw Amelia

Lily revealed as the act voted to return by the public vote, as had been widely expected. She actually received nearly 50 per cent of votes, so she returned with a solid mandate. Her return was one of two big talking points for the show – the other being a 16-minute delay in the start of the show after a power surge at BT Tower interrupted the broadcast just as it was due to begin. Archived first-round auditions were shown to baffled viewers, as pandemonium broke out around Tulisa and her fellow judges, with producers desperately trying to get the show back on track as soon as possible. Once the show began, Tulisa looked forward to introducing Little Mix. When she did so, she described them as 'my little muffins – Little Mix'. After their performance of the Lady Gaga song 'Telephone', they received essentially positive feedback from Walsh and Rowland, despite the latter saying they needed to 'tighten up their harmonies'. It was Barlow who really turned on them. 'Girls, I feel a little bit disappointed in you tonight,' he began prompting boos and jeers from the audience. Barlow said it was not their performance that made him feel let down, but he felt they had become 'predictable'. Turning to Tulisa, he said: 'It feels like you're running out of ideas for these girls.'

Tulisa naturally leapt to their – and indeed her own – defence. However, Barlow had not finished turning the screw. He interrupted Tulisa's defence, and turned to Little Mix to ask: 'Do you want to do something different?' As the band members responded by shuffling and looking anxiously at one another, he said: 'I think you do.' Tulisa explained that 'whatever anyone on this panel says' she was proud of the girls and felt they deserved credit. She then appealed directly to the residents of the regions the girls came from to shore up the vote. 'I want Newcastle to pick up the phone, I want High Wycombe to pick up the phone, I want Essex to pick up the phone,' she said, and, beating the table to emphasise her point, she added: 'and I want them to vote for Little Mix!' After the results show, Tulisa let her hair down with another Sunday evening out. She joined her former act The Risk and the comedic Johnny Robinson at the G.A.Y. nightclub. Wearing a glamorous, sequinned white dress, she looked superb as she supported both acts. Later in the night, Aussie pop legend Gina G took to the stage to bring a thoroughly camp night to a Eurovisionesque conclusion. As for Tulisa, she continued the party at the exclusive Modiva nightclub later on.

Controversy was never far away in this series of *The X Factor*, and Tulisa was almost continually right in the thick of it. Following Misha B's second placing in the bottom two, the act herself was asked why she thought she had again polled so few votes. She referred back to the remarks that Tulisa and Walsh had made some weeks ago about her behaviour backstage, saying: 'I think because of some of the past allegations that were made on previous shows ... I think that has had an effect on the public and I just think I'm misunderstood to some sort of extent.' It seemed that Tulisa's public vow that she and Misha had settled their differences would not be enough to end the controversy. Nor, judging by the Tulisa-centric media reports that ran with Misha's statement, would it ever be widely recalled that it was Walsh and not Tulisa that made the most damning accusation against Misha.

However, the harshest words being exchanged in the aftermath of the show were between Tulisa and Barlow. The reverberations of his criticisms of Little Mix continued when he explained later: 'They had great vocals but what I want to see is something different. Then Tulisa let it slip in the corridor that they will be doing something different next week, so OK, fair enough, now she's listening to me.' Tulisa was quick to shoot back at him. 'His ego is out of control, isn't it?' she said. 'Gary could have a party with his ego, he really could. We should have a birthday party just for his ego.'

Later, unnamed sources were claimed to have underscored her angry remarks by confirming she was furious with Barlow for interfering with her mentorship of Little Mix. Certainly, it had been a week of direct interventions by him. He had also savaged Janet Devlin in his assessment of her performance. It is always tricky to call which judges' spats are genuine and which are engineered purely to add a bit of spice to the show. Indeed, for the judges themselves it is sometimes a curious combination of the two. Reports of a falling-out between Rowland and her act Janet were of more substance and consequence. It was said that Devlin was no longer speaking to her mentor, who she felt was prioritising Misha B over her. Certainly, Devlin's increasingly moody behaviour on-screen and the death stares she sometimes gave out on-stage suggested that she was troubled by something. It was all a far cry from the sweet girl who performed 'Your Song' at her first audition.

As for Tulisa and her remaining act Little Mix, their relationship was perhaps the strongest mentor/act rapport of the series. Having steered them through another week of the public vote, Tulisa had already made them the most successful girl band in *X Factor* history, as none had ever lasted as far into the competition as Little Mix had. Could they, people began to wonder, go all the way to the final and then win? The fact that a girl band was even being spoken of as potential winners was a huge credit to Little Mix and, of course, to Tulisa herself. Meanwhile, 'sources' quoted in various publications suggested various scenarios going on backstage at *The X Factor*, many of which reportedly involved Tulisa. One report in the *Mirror* claimed that Devlin was convinced that both Tulisa and Barlow 'had it in for her' and were ganging up to get her voted out of the competition. It was claimed that her mentor Rowland shared the concern and had told Devlin to prepare to be in the bottom two soon. Whether Devlin was suffering from any such paranoia was a moot point: more important was that any such fears would surely be misplaced. The problem Devlin faced was that her vocal style was ill suited for a competition such as *The X Factor*, with its fixed themes for each live show. Pre-emptively blaming Tulisa for a bottom-two placing that had yet to transpire was absurd. Another theory doing the rounds was that Tulisa was afraid that the ongoing controversy about Misha B was costing her acts votes. Still shocked at the premature departure of The Risk, Tulisa had reportedly begun to fear that her acts were being punished in the public vote due to anger over her comments to Misha B. The fact that Walsh – who had also criticised Misha – had lost all his acts since, and that she had just one act remaining might have added mathematical credence to this theory, but it seemed a speculation too far. Indeed, Little Mix were said to have reassured her that they did not believe they would suffer as a result of the Misha saga.

There was good news for Tulisa's partner, Fazer, when he was chosen by Simon Cowell to produce what would become the winner's single. 'I'll be producing for the *X Factor* winner, it's been decided,' he told the *Sun* in November. 'This isn't just a hook-up with Tulisa, I'm going to work with whichever act wins. I've been talking to SyCo [Cowell's joint venture with Sony] about working on a few different things for them.' This development followed on the heels of Fazer writing a song for American pop star Katy Perry, which he hoped she might record and released in 2012. He felt his growing stature as a songwriter, together with his influences, tastes and directions, made him a formidable prospect for the *X Factor* winner's single. With a number of outside acts lining up to challenge the eventual *X Factor* winner for the Christmas No 1, Fazer realised the states were high. For him, originality was key. 'We really want to give a new flavour to the *X Factor* acts,' he said. 'It's going to suit me. I have rock influences, hip-hop, pop, whatever. I have produced Dappy's new track and songs for Tulisa too. I'm hoping for the Christmas Nos 1 and 2.'

Meanwhile, Tulisa was preparing to perform at Gary Barlow's charity extravaganza, the Children In Need Rocks Manchester show at the MEN Arena. With thousands watching at the venue and millions more following from home via the BBC, this was a huge event. For Tulisa, as well as the charitable dimension, it was also a chance to show those who had only come to know of her as an *X Factor* judge that she is, first and foremost, a musical performer. Gary Barlow explained how she had become such a central figure in his Children In Need project. 'Tulisa is on the main chorus and she sounds great,' he said. 'It's great for us she's not got a record out for Christmas. She's going to be a massive star. My working relationship with her is brilliant, really good. When the idea of this came up, I thought, "Well, I'm on a chair next to her most of the day, so I'll just ask her." And she was totally up for it straight away. She's a really instinctive girl. She knows immediately whether she likes something or not.'

Tulisa wore a black waistcoat top and black leggings with a sparkling design down the sides of each leg as she took to the stage to deliver the chorus of a song called 'Teardrop', performed by an ensemble of mostly urban acts dubbed The Collective. The gathering included Dot Rotten, Tinchy Stryder, Rizzle Kicks, Ms Dynamite, Mz Bratt, Labrinth, Wretch 32 and Ed Sheeran. . It was a fine start to an exciting evening. Tulisa sang her parts well enough, but seemed nervous and almost overly serious.

Later in the show, Tulisa's N-Dubz band-mates appeared and sang 'No Regrets'. At one point, Dappy jumped down in the trench between the stage and the front row of the audience. He was quickly bundled back to the stage – this was a charity event being broadcast on none other than the BBC, after all!

By the end of the night Tulisa and the rest of the stellar bill – which included queen of pop Lady Gaga – had put on a fine show and raised plenty of money for charity. It had been an enjoyable night and an important one. Those involved in *The X Factor* can lose sight of the world beyond that talent show. As Barlow said: 'It's been nice to concentrate on something other than *X Factor*. We're in a bubble down there. It's been good to leave London. We get tied up with our own importance.' His words will have rung true for Tulisa, surely. Tulisa then had less than 48 hours until the next live show. It had been an eventful week, including a trip to the premiere of the much-anticipated *Breaking Dawn* movie, which is the fifth instalment of the popular *Twilight* series. She confirmed which of the two lead males of the film she is most fond of, when asked that perennial *Twilight* question: are you Team Edward or Team Jacob? 'Team Jacob all the way,' she said. 'He's just got that mysterious vibe going on in the film, like a dark horse. I like dark characters.'

Little Mix's performance of En Vogue's 'Don't Let Go' was superb. The song, taken from the soundtrack of the film *Set It Off*, really suited them. All four judges were full of praise. Tulisa said, 'Girls, can I just take the time to express to the nation how proud I am. You really went for it tonight.'

Her pride was quite understandable. Rowland had told them: 'You could be the best girl group to come out of the UK' and Barlow added, 'That was your best performance to date – brilliant!' It was enough to get them through to the final five – the first time a girl band had managed such a feat in the history of *The X Factor*. Reaching the eighth week of the series meant they had surpassed the previous record, held by the Conway Sisters who reached week seven back in 2005. Their own charm and musical talent, together with Tulisa's willingness to push the 'girl power' button when she spoke about them, had combined to put them among the favourites to win. 'Tulisa is a brilliant mentor,' said Jesy Nelson afterwards. 'She is so full on and she does everything for us. She is not only our mentor, she is our friend.' With her beloved act through to the quarter-final and no major rows or disagreements taking place during the weekend, it had been a satisfying round of live shows for her and her act.

Even though Tulisa had been essentially out of the key dramas of the weekend's show, she was thrust straight back into the limelight within days of Craig Colton's exit. The arm gesture with which she opened many shows came under the spotlight of a media regulator following complaints from viewers. During each episode, provided she was wearing short sleeves, Tulisa would lift her right arm and wink as she was introduced by host Dermot O'Leary. Tattooed across her arm is 'The Female Boss' –

also the name of her perfume. The broadcasting regulator Ofcom reportedly opened an investigation into whether she was breaking television rules. Following suggestions she had been fishing for freebies when she had plugged products during interviews a few months back, this was a story Tulisa could do without.

There were precedents of Ofcom coming down hard on *X Factor* figures. In January 2011, Ofcom had found *The X Factor* in breach of product placement rules after presenter Dermot O'Leary appeared to encourage viewers to download songs by guest acts Diana Vickers and Michael Bublé. In 2010, Ofcom had received almost 3,000 complaints about sexualised dance routines by Rihanna and Christina Aguilera during last year's *X Factor* finals. Ofcom warned the show it was skating on thin ice with such raunchy routines. These are just two of the Ofcom investigations that have taken place into *X Factor* matters. As one wag commented: 'The X Factor must keep Ofcom in their jobs.' So Tulisa could expect that censure was possible. However, in public she came out defiant and fighting. 'I was showing off my tattoo long before *The X Factor*,' she told the *Mirror*. 'It's always been my trademark and it's always been my nickname. The perfume's not actually called The Female Boss – it's just TFB. So someone wouldn't go into a shop and buy my perfume just because they'd seen my tattoo. The show told me it's OK, I can carry on doing it – and I will.' She was good to her word, continuing to perform the arm salute whenever she was wearing short-sleeved outfits that revealed her forearms.

Then *Closer* magazine claimed to lift the lid on behind-the-scenes stresses and traumas being suffered by Tulisa. All the claims in the magazine were attributed only to unnamed 'insiders' and 'pals'. The story claimed that Tulisa considered her decision to join *The X Factor* one of the 'biggest mistakes' of her life. The row with Rowland was still very much an ongoing concern, said the story, which also claimed the American had called Tulisa a 'nobody' backstage and that the two judges now left the studio half an hour apart. Another claim was that Tulisa had blown her top after discovering Gary Barlow had been having secret meetings with Cheryl Cole in a bid to lure her back to the judging panel. The reported effect on Tulisa was profound: she was said to be having sleepless nights, surviving on coffee and even having a panic attack backstage immediately prior to a live show. 'She doesn't know how much longer she can cope,' said *Closer*'s 'source'.

However, anyone who had seen Tulisa's confident, smiley and shining entrances to each live show would be hard pushed to believe that she had recently been suffering from any sort of serious discomfort. It was best to take these claims with a pinch of salt, though it is certainly true that the stresses and pressures of being an *X Factor* judge and mentor have often knocked the confidence of those in the famous chairs. Sharon Osbourne, Dannii Minogue, Louis Walsh and Cheryl Cole had all spoken at some point in the past about how tough and stressful they found the task. Only Simon Cowell had never complained about life on the show – but then it is his party. The previous week,

Tulisa had told *Heat* magazine that she was 'finding it stressful' and admitted that there were 'times when it does get a bit too much'. However, these admissions fell short of the apocalyptic suggestions in *Closer*'s article.

As the *Closer* report was published Tulisa had half her professional imagination on a non-*X Factor* related front. 'We're putting out a greatest hits record on 28th November which I hope the fans – new and old – will love,' she said when she announced the release in an earlier interview. Included among the 18 tracks were obvious choices such as 'I Need You', 'We Dance On' and 'Best Behaviour'. The album also features covers of the Sugababes' 'About You Now' and The Script's 'The Man Who Can't Be Moved', in addition to an 'N-Dubz version' of Dappy's solo single 'No Regrets'. Tulisa's mention of 'new' N-Dubz fans showed how hopeful the band was that her *X Factor* fame would lead to extra sales for them, as millions of people previously unaware or only distantly familiar with the band noticed them for the first time. Such were the extra benefits of the mass exposure N-Dubz were given thanks to her place in *The X Factor*.

As the next Saturday evening show opened there was intensified interest in Tulisa's entrance, as viewers wondered if she would repeat her arm salute following the complaints to Ofcom. Sure enough, she did repeat the gesture. This time, she had cheekily added – in pen – a message on her left arm too. It read 'Vote Little Mix!'

Little Mix opened the show with a mash-up of 'Baby' by Justin Bieber and 'Chain Reaction' by Diana Ross. They received mixed comments from the judges but their second performance was showered with praise. They sang 'Beautiful' by Christina Aguilera. The performance had added intensity as Jesy in particular had been targeted online about her appearance. She said: 'When I sing this song, I get quite emotional as it reminds me of the insecurities I went through when I was younger.' They sang the song, well, *beautifully*, as their individual vocal talent shone through. By the end of the performance a few of the band were in tears and so was Kelly Rowland. No doubt plenty of viewers were, also. 'Girls, you pulled it out of the bag for your second song,' said Walsh. 'It's amazing to see a girl band with four lead vocals. Tulisa, I would love to see these girls in the final.' After the tearful Rowland and the impressed Barlow also delivered their verdict it was time for proud Tulisa to praise her 'little muffins'. 'To me that was your best performance of the series,' she said, adding her boisterous encouragement to viewers to vote for Little Mix. Certainly, the band could not conceivably have given greater incentive for viewers to do so than they did with their second song.

As the public voted over the following 24 hours, it was hard for any of the acts and their respective mentors to feel confident. Of the remaining acts only Misha B and Amelia had previously been in the bottom two. Therefore, both were vulnerable to another sing-off positioning. However, both had been particularly strong on the night. Equally, while the 'Irish vote' had seemed to be firmly behind Janet, she had stumbled so badly during her first song that it was easy to imagine her falling. As for Little Mix, they seemed strong but had performed in the unfancied opening slot of the show. Also, while they could take pride that they had already lasted longer than any other girl band, they were also all too aware that such a trend-bucking run could end. Perhaps only Marcus had no specific cause for pessimism. Consequently, there was a particularly tense atmosphere at the results show on Sunday night. Tulisa appeared with the rest of the judges as usual. She looked sensational in a figure-hugging sheer black dress. Her beautiful curves were shown off to the full in the eye-catching outfit. This time she did not perform the arm salute, but only because her outfit had long sleeves which covered her tattoo. The two performing acts were *X Factor* graduate Olly Murs and Jessie J. During the latter's post-song chat with Dermot she saluted the efforts of Tulisa, who she had assisted at the judges' houses phase. Asked who she wanted to win she did not dodge the question as so many guests disappointingly do. Instead she proudly declared 'Little Mix!' much to Tulisa's delight.

There was even greater delight for Tulisa when the results of the public vote were revealed later in the show. The tension was almost unbearable as Little Mix remained on the stage after Dermot had put through Amelia and Marcus. With just one more automatic place remaining in the semi-final, all three remaining acts – Little Mix, Janet and Misha B – were staring at a place in the dreaded sing-offs. As Dermot paused before revealing the final act to go straight through, the tension on Tulisa's face was clear. The crowd began to chant 'Little Mix! Little Mix!' Then Dermot announced Little Mix's name and she and her band celebrated in style. Leaping and punching the air, their joy and passion made for an emotional sight. Their screams of disbelieving joy were also powerful. The following morning, one newspaper would focus bitchily on Tulisa's celebration but for the moment she was simply lost in her joy, pride and relief. Soon, tears were flowing from her eyes. If anybody wanted a symbolic slice of evidence at how competitive Tulisa is and how seriously she took her role as a mentor, this was it. She and her 'little muffins' remained celebrating on the stage long after programme etiquette would dictate they should have left, to allow the sing-off to start. She was so proud.

Afterwards, she told the *Sun* why she thought the band was so successfully bucking the trend of girl bands on the show. 'Little Mix are sweet, cute and fresh,' she said. 'They're not like N-Dubz. They are endearing. They don't seem like the kind of girls who are going to nick your boyfriend. They're the kind of girls whose shoulder you want to cry on.' There would be more tears to come for Tulisa and her act. Happily, they would be tears of joy as she fulfilled her dream of becoming the first *X Factor* mentor to take a group all the way to the final. Naturally, the journey there would not be entirely smooth. This was Tulisa and *The X Factor*, after all.

CHAPTER
TEN

Having taken Little Mix through to the semi-final and fended off the row about her 'arm gesture', Tulisa might have hoped that she could be out of the firing line for a while. Surely all the controversy was behind her? No chance: in the wake of the quarter-final weekend she was once more in the thick of things as the Misha B row was ignited yet again, this time by the contestant herself. 'Why the whole thing was brought up was never really explained... they just went from being about the music to being about nonsense,' Misha B told a newspaper. She went on to put the blame on her poor showing in the voting directly on the comments made by Tulisa and Walsh some weeks previously. 'I know if I was watching the show and someone accused someone like they did without knowing the facts then that would make me change my mind on the person. I understand how people think and how as human beings they are heavily influenced by people's comments. Of course it is going to damage my chances of winning the show,' said Misha B. 'It got blown so out of proportion and the judges weren't there and jumped to conclusions.'

As these reports again dragged Tulisa into the centre of the story despite Walsh's comparatively harsher observations, she also woke up to jibes about her Sunday evening dress in the *Daily Mail*. TULISA HITS A BUM NOTE AS HER SHEER DRESS LEAVES LITTLE TO THE IMAGINATION ON X FACTOR, ran the headline. The story went on to explain how 'under the bright studio lights' her backside was visible when she jumped for joy celebrating Little Mix's progression to the semi-finals. To give the story more foundation, it repeated a vow Tulisa had made the previous week to never pose nude in a magazine, however lucrative the offer. 'I'd never get naked in a mag,' she had said. 'I don't care how much money. You can offer me millions. I'm not a prostitute. I'm sorry, naked? That's no diss to anyone who does it, but I'm a musician – I'm not selling my body.' However, there was a growing army of male fans who would love her to peel off her clothes in a magazine. Her soaring popularity among the men of Britain could have made Fazer jealous. He took it as a compliment, however. 'I love it that guys fancy her and want to get with her,' he told *Heat*. 'It's far better than them saying, "Fazer, what the f*** are you doing with her?!"It's good.'

Tulisa, speaking in the same week to *Glamour* magazine,

said she *does* have a possessive streak. 'I get jealous,' she said of her feelings for Fazer. 'If he's seeing his girl mates, I want to know them. I say, "What friend? You don't need female friends. Why didn't I know her before? Introduce me. Let's go out for dinner".' She went on to describe how she considered herself to be as a girlfriend. A lot of the qualities she described were ones that many men would find hard to live with. At least, though, she was honest and frank when she said: 'I don't stand for any sh*te. I'm selfish. I'm very stubborn. I never back down and I'm possessive.' If any of her words were causing alarm bells to ring in the minds of men who fancied her, she balanced these statements with descriptions of more admirable traits. 'But I'm very accommodating,' she continued. 'If he has a problem we talk about what we can do to fix it.' If she was coming across as a coin with two sides, that was intentional, as that is how she sees herself. 'If you fight me, I'm a raging bull,' she said, adding: 'If you work with me, I'm good at that. And I'm very snugly.' She gave the final word to Fazer, when she quoted his favourite assessment of her. 'As he always says, one minute I'm a puppy dog, the next I'm the ice queen,' she said.

The jealous side which she alluded to in that interview had shown itself in October when she took to Twitter to launch a fuming online invective in response to a woman she felt had tried to be a little too friendly to her boyfriend. She wrote: '2all women! don't mess with my man! I may b famous but I will still cum and whup ur ass if u under-estimate me! don't b disrespectful' (sic). In a separate

Tweet, she added: 'MGW [money grabbing wh*re] women make me laugh, NO darlin not only is he not interested but he came straight back n told me LHFAO bout u, years ago it wuda been hot.' After a period of silence, she returned to the site to say she was in a mood to 'cause trouble' and that she wanted to explain her previous 'rant'. She wrote: '4 the record that rant was directed at a girl tryin it on with my fella who she knows is with me! WELL DESERVED'.

Meanwhile Tulisa was beginning to look beyond *The X Factor* and was planning a well-earned winter getaway once her duties on the show were complete. The one place she said she would not be going to was Barbados, where Simon Cowell and other celebrities jet to most winters. 'I wanna get away from all that but still go some place where I know someone 'cos I hate going away and not knowing my way around,' she told the *Mirror*. 'Wherever I go there's got to be beautiful scenery... and something to do.' Ironically she would, as we shall see, go to Barbados after all. Between shows she continued her partying ways. In addition to her regular jaunts at G.A.Y. she let her hair down at other venues, including the Jalouse nightclub in London, where she joined celebrations for rapper Chipmunk's 21st birthday. Alongside her were several cast members of what she says is 'her favourite television show of all time', *The Only Way Is Essex*. Wearing a white mini dress with gold and silver embellishment and black patent heels, she danced, partied and drank the night away. The next morning she seemed to have second thoughts about her previous evening's online activity, when she Tweeted: 'I am deleting every tweet I sent last night simply cus I don't remember sending them hahaha.' Oh, to have seen the content of the Tweets in question before she deleted them.

Meanwhile, discussion turned to which acts would duet with the *X Factor* finalists in the weekend of final shows. In the past such musical royalty as Robbie Williams, Beyoncé, Christina Aguilera and Rihanna had sung alongside individual finalists. The speculation over who would appear this time had already begun, with Coldplay rumoured to have been approached. When Little Mix was asked by a journalist who they most wanted to duet with should they reach the final, Perrie said: 'Tulisa!' It would be an *X Factor* first if a finalist were to duet with their mentor. Jesy added: 'She is so passionate about us. We're so close to her and I just love her to pieces.' On the duet issue, it was believed that Tulisa was interested in such an arrangement but feared it might cause tension among the other judges.

In any case, she reminded her act, they had to get through the semi-final and earn public vote to join the final line-up before any choice for a duet could be officially finalised. Having dampened their expectations one day she raised them the following day when she claimed that *X Factor* supremo Simon Cowell had told her that he predicted Little Mix would win the final. 'He told me that he really liked the girls,' she said. 'He actually said he's backing them to win.' A vote of confidence from the genius behind the *X Factor* franchise – and whose presence in the UK shows was sorely missed – was a significant boost for

Tulisa's girl band. It was a boost that was probably needed, as a simultaneous story was published claiming that band member Perrie Edwards was dating One Direction boy Zayn Malik. Could such a rumour lead to the boy band's famously fanatical following turning against Little Mix out of jealousy? Only weeks earlier *Xtra Factor* presenter Caroline Flack had witnessed how harsh such backlashes can be when she received death threats and a tidal wave of abuse after it was rumoured she had dated One Direction's ever-popular Harry Styles.

A less glamorous but in many ways more important development for Tulisa came in the shape of an award that recognised her contribution to awareness about mental health issues. She won a Media Award from the mental health charity Mind for the documentary *Tulisa: My Mum And Me*. She told the ceremony at the British Film Institute in London how proud she was. 'Mental health issues are something that's very close to my heart,' she said. 'Winning a Mind Media Award means so much to me, I'm blown away. It's something that affects so many people and their families. I wanted *My Mum And Me* to show that no one should be ashamed to speak out about mental health issues.' A rep from the production company praised Tulisa's frankness. 'Tulisa and all our contributors were so open about sharing their stories. It's an honour to pay tribute to such strong, young and resilient carers and to bring to light just how hard they work to make day to day life more bearable for those they look after.'

It was a mark of what an important public figure Tulisa

was becoming that within the space of seven days she was so ubiquitous in the public eye and that her high profile came through several channels. As well as her ongoing *X Factor* position she was also in the charts with the N-Dubz *Greatest Hits* album, in the gossip magazines due to her celebrity coupling with Fazer, and also winning a prestigious award from a mental health charity. From an essentially frivolous reality television show through power-coupling and a leading urban band to charity worthiness, Tulisa was proving to be quite the versatile celebrity. With her branded perfume in the shops for Christmas and talk of a novel and solo career in 2012, she could not be accused of putting all her eggs in one basket.

The semi-final weekend was truly eventful, as the 2011 *X Factor* series really sprang into life near the close. As in the previous week, each remaining act sang two songs: the first with a Motown theme, the second under the banner of 'the song to get me into the final'. The stakes had never been higher. There to support Tulisa was one special fan: her mother Ann. Tulisa had revealed Ann's presence at the studios on Twitter, earlier in the evening. She wrote: 'Gettin ready 4 2nits show, mums in the dressing room with me givin me mummy support lol!Ive got butterflies! Fingers crossed 4#LITTLEMIX'. Forever the daughter playing the mother role, Tulisa was supporting her mother just when she might have expected to be the one receiving the support.

Little Mix sang 'You Keep Me Hangin' On' by The Supremes as their Motown song. The comments from

Walsh and Rowland were positive, but Barlow's feedback was more incisive. 'Perrie is actually the best singer in this band,' he stated. 'I think she should be featured a lot more than she is. That's what missing at the moment for me, a focus, a lead singer.' Tulisa showed her disgust in her facial expressions, even before verbally responding to Barlow's remarks. 'What Little Mix represent are four different people who, when they come together, are four strong individuals,' she said. 'They love each other and want to give each other as much time on the record.' For their 'song to get them into the final', Little Mix chose 'If I Were A Boy', by Beyoncé. The intensity of the moment was clear in the facial expressions of the band members. Their concentrated gazes and synchronised bobbing as they sang made for a moving performance. Walsh compared them to Girls Aloud, pointing out it was 10 years since that band had emerged after being assembled on *Popstars: The Rivals*. Rowland told them that if they could 'find the strength within each other' they would be able to 'change the world'. Gary, though, was less impressed. He told them they were 'not good enough tonight'.

To say this lit the touch-paper in Tulisa's mind would be an understatement. Finally unleashing her N-Dubz self on the show, she thumped the table hard as she pleaded for people to vote for Little Mix and continued thumping away as she roared that they 'deserve to win the competition!' It was an amazingly powerful outburst. Never in *X Factor* history had a judge shouted so loud for their act. Nor had there ever been any incident of such violent desk-thumping. Tulisa had raised eyebrows across the studio. She later had a bit of fun on Twitter, writing: 'Wow! My hand hurts... Save our little muffins.' The voters did just that, and Tulisa's band was safely through to the final. Not only that, they went into the final as the favourites in the eyes of a significant number of viewers and commentators.

In the wake of her historic achievement, Tulisa faced another onslaught of negative stories, the foundation of some of them spurious to say the least. First, the *Daily Mail* claimed that when Tulisa cried during Misha B's farewell song that the tears had been motivated by guilt. Its headline screamed that she had fought back 'tears of guilt' as if this was fact. The story went on to claim: 'Perhaps feeling guilty at her part in the Misha bullying scandal, Tulisa was seen weeping as she worked her way through the song.' Perhaps, indeed – or perhaps not. More likely is that Tulisa was caught-up in all the emotions of the moment: pride and relief that her act had made the final, sadness at the exit of Misha B – an act that she admired musically and who of all in the competition had come most from her neck of the musical woods.

As for Misha B, later that same day she confirmed that there was no remaining tension on her part when it came to Tulisa. Asked on *Daybreak* if she had forgiven Tulisa, she said: 'Forgiving is the thing that I have done. I believe that in situations that occur in life, you shouldn't get bitter you should just get better.' The Mancunian added: 'Because there's a saying that to forgive is to set a prisoner free, and I realised that prisoner was me. And instead of getting bitter about a situation – because it's only making you not feel good inside. And for that situation I'm so grateful because it has been one of the greatest experiences of my life – for me to look at the situation and grow and learn from it. I'm just so grateful.' That was by no means the only interview she gave in the 24 hours following her *X Factor* exit in which she was given the opportunity to blame her downfall on Tulisa. Given the undoubted massive talent she had, which had been clear for all to see from her first audition to her farewell song with its original rap lines, she was under pressure to provide a sound bite with which the media could explain why she was no longer in the competition. It was refreshing to see Misha B resist so many times the temptation to turn on Tulisa. She also, incidentally, resisted the opportunity to slam Barlow, who had told her on the Saturday show that the bullying claim meant she could not win the show. 'I've got the utmost respect for Gary – I think he's amazing,' said Misha, who was showing admirable restraint as she was bombarded with leading questions. She added: 'understand what he was saying.' Asked who she wanted to win the show, she chose Little Mix, and spoke with glowing approval of Tulisa's act. She said if they did not win she would like Marcus Collins to take the title. Anyone other than Amelia Lily, in other words?

With talk of a 'feud' between her and Misha seemingly laid to rest, Tulisa could look forward to putting the much-hyped story behind her. Except that the following morning's *Daily Star* had the headline *X FACTOR* SLURS RUINED LIFE, above a story about Misha B. An unnamed 'source' claimed that Misha had snubbed Tulisa, Walsh and Barlow after the results show on Sunday, claiming: 'She is convinced they wrecked her hopes in this show, and future deals, in a very calculated way.' The veracity of the source was questionable, not least in the light of the pains Misha to which had gone the previous day in order to diffuse the issue. Indeed, the only significant direct quote on the matter the *Daily Star* story included about Misha was: 'What they said had an effect. I think it did have an effect.'

On the same day, a more authentic story appeared on the *Heatworld* website, in which Misha B said – in a video interview – that she was 'grateful' for the experience she had with Tulisa. She said it had helped her to mature 'as a person'. In case of any remaining doubt over how she felt, she said she found Tulisa 'inspirational – I've nothing bad to say about her.' It does not get much clearer than that. It is easy to dismiss the entire saga as just another of those *X Factor* spats that get hyped to the hilt to keep the show in the headlines and therefore in the public eye. While it had a flavour of that to it, for Tulisa it was far more significant. With *The X Factor* under intense scrutiny due to the absence of Simon Cowell and the introduction of the new judging panel, it would be easy for any of the new judges – or the very show itself – to fall irrevocably from public view. Scepticism over the concept of a televised talent contest had started to grow. The slightest hint of exploitation by judges of what are always perceived to be entirely vulnerable contestants could be deadly for the personality involved. Tulisa had been hired for her feisty nature, so she was particularly vulnerable to such accusations. Mindful of the 'vile chav' talk that greeted her appointment, it was even more important for her to not be embroiled in any unpleasant allegations.

Then, there was the second post-semi-final storm for her to weather. She simultaneously faced a new plugging row, when she was criticised for using her Twitter account to promote a dental firm that had given her free tooth veneers. Having been fitted with 12 porcelain veneers by dentist Dr David Bloom at Senova Dental in Watford, Hertfordshire, free of charge after she was hired as an *X Factor* judge, Tulisa had been overjoyed with her new look. She told the *Radio Times* how happy she was to be on the receiving end of so many 'freebies' since coming under the *X Factor* umbrella. 'It's mental, the amount of free things I get offered,' she said. 'There are things I work to afford and I don't have to pay for them. It's ridiculous. I could sell half the free things I have and be able to put a mortgage down on a house.'

The press then suggested that she might be facing an Office of Fair Trading (OFT) investigation for her mentions on Twitter of how and where she had received her veneers. She had first mentioned the treatment on Twitter in March, when she Tweeted on one of her treatment days, signing off the message 'THANK U...DAVID!xx' She subsequently sent out four further

Tweets about the treatment, each name-checking the dental firm that had given her the treatment. One such message, sent during the summer, read: 'Every1 keeps asking me about my new teeth & who did them, so here goes @drdavidbloom @senovadental, their [they're] amazing so happy.' The fact Tulisa had not mentioned that she had received the treatment free of charge meant she risked falling foul of OFT regulations. The organisation, which does not publicly confirm whether an individual is being investigated, stated: 'It must be clear if endorsements in blogs, posts and microblogs like Twitter have been made in return for payment or payment in kind.'

The week leading up to *The X Factor* final is normally one of relentless hype, excitement and expectation. In 2011 the anticipation took a while to get going. The first major story of the week centred around an apparent mistake on the website of music chain HMV. A 'winners single' for Amelia Lily appeared on the website, leading to claims that here was a 'smoking gun' proving the show was fixed for her to win it. The chain was forced to apologise, saying that 'an unforeseen and regrettable technical issue' had caused the page to appear. Conspiracy theorists were scarcely placated by HMV's words. As well as those who claimed the mistake showed that victory had been fixed for Lily, others claimed that this was evidence of a plot to destroy her. This theory posited that the story had been cooked up to discredit Lily and therefore push more votes to Little Mix, the supposed beneficiaries of the fix in this scenario. Twitter users raged, using the hashtag 'fix factor'.

However, a more positive sense of excitement surrounded the announcement, 48 hours before the final, that Tulisa, Barlow and Rowland would duet with their respective acts in the final. As we have seen, the duet is a key part of the final. The news that the three judges would duet with their acts gave the 2011 final a new dimension. Asked how she felt about the prospect of her duet with Little Mix, Tulisa said: 'I'm more nervous than they are!' There was much laughter as Barlow observed: 'Thank God Louis didn't get an act in the final.' Walsh took the quip in good heart and said: 'I think Johnny [Robinson] and I would have been a good duet... We were thinking of Renée and Renato, "Save Your Love".' Tulisa was wonderfully ebullient about the chances for her act in the final. *The X Factor* is not a forum for false modesty or shy understatement and she was not in the mood for either. 'A group has never won this competition, especially not a girl group even getting this far in the competition,' she said. 'I'm the youngest judge, it's my first year and I want to change *X Factor* history with these little muffins behind me.' On a more personal note, she also reflected on the impact the series had wrought on her. 'It has been a journey and very life-consuming,' she said. Fellow judge Barlow had also recently spoken of what a toll the duties had taken on him. That a man with as long and at times tumultuous showbiz career as Barlow found it a strain is significant. For Tulisa, who had seen plenty of drama in her life but who was younger and fresher, it was also a trial. 'It does become your world,' she said. 'Literally. It takes over your life.'

Turning to the much-discussed tears she had shed while watching Misha B's exit from the semi-final, Tulisa explained that despite her reputation as a hard character, she too could hurt sometimes. 'I am not a stone,' she said. 'If I see someone going through such an emotional thing, it's hard not to be upset at that. I completely get it. I can imagine how they must feel. I felt very emotional watching her journey and it just ended. If anyone had been in that position I would be crying.' She said another factor in her emotions was the knowledge, as she watched Misha's farewell performance, that it could have been her own 'little muffins' waving goodbye. 'I thought this journey could be over and that scared the crap out of me to the point where I was tearful before I came on,' she said. 'Then just seeing Misha go made it real... that a contestant that had been in a competition for that long is now going home.'

As for Tulisa's band members, they embarked on the traditional 'journey home' that finalists make in the week after the semi-final. It makes for a powerful 'VT' video to be run prior to their performance on the big final. Jane told reporters that their beloved mentor was making sure they kept their feet on the ground, despite being spoken of as many people's favourites to win the show and then build a worthwhile career afterwards. 'There is no way we will become divas,' she said. 'It's just not our style. We'd give each other a slap. Tulisa keeps us grounded and we all keep each other very grounded, too.'

Tulisa took the chance to take a swipe at rival judge

Gary Barlow. The Take That singer had heavily criticised Little Mix in the semi-final. Tulisa felt this was no coincidence. '[Gary's comment] was tactical – 100 per cent,' she told the *Mirror*. 'If they win this competition they could become a brand like the Spice Girls – everyone has their favourite member, so everyone needs their time to shine. There will be a little girl at home waiting for a certain one to come on.' Cleverly, she then positioned Little Mix as the plucky underdogs of the final showdown. 'All the odds are stacked against us – I'm up against Mr Competitive in Gary Barlow and a girl band has never won,' she said. 'But the other part of me says things were against N-Dubz and we made it. We are in the final, but we are still the underdogs. I just hope the underdogs can win.'

It was the sentiment of the N-Dubz album *Against All Odds* transferred to her new gig. Playing the underdog card was a shrewd move. Tulisa is unlikely to become a politician any time soon but she had shown throughout the *X Factor* live shows that she can electioneer with the best of them. Thumping the desk as she implored each of the girls' home towns to 'pick up the phone and vote for them', presenting them as a force for good in society, and then placing them as the underdogs of the final weekend – she was pushing some very effective buttons with the audience. Would it be enough to see her become the youngest-ever winning mentor in *X Factor* history, and enough for the act to become the first band to win the competition? The closest any band had come before was the second-placed finish for G4 and JLS, and then the third-placefor One Direction.

Meanwhile, having told her act to remain focused and keep their feet on the ground, Tulisa had to stay grounded herself when, just days before the *X Factor* final, she was voted ahead of Kate Middleton and boy band One Direction in a poll of young people to find Britain's 'most magical people'. She was the highest-ranking celebrity in the poll, finishing just behind 'Mum' at number one and 'Dad' at number two. The survey was carried out among 1,000 young people aged 4 to 16 years old on behalf of the Lite Sprites toys. While such polls should be kept in perspective as a bit of fun and are only partially representative at best, it remained a welcome boost to her to her spirits know that she was rated so highly among young people. Indeed, the news was also further vindication of Simon Cowell's selection of her to make *The X Factor* appeal to younger viewers. He had, it was widely felt, got many things wrong for the 2011 series of the show but hiring Tulisa was proving to be the wisest stroke he had pulled. As he remained in America, trying to pull *X Factor USA* closer towards the sort of viewing figures he had envisaged for it, he decided after all to not join the panel for the final of the British show. It was felt he had decided that the best thing for him was not to be associated too closely with this latest, controversial, instalment of the show. However, he remained very proud of Tulisa and the contribution she had made. Hiring 'Trouble' had, he felt, been a great move.

If she could steer Little Mix to victory, Tulisa would consider the experience to have been particularly successful. As she prepared for the final hurdle of the long series, she looked back not only over her *X Factor* experiences but over her career and life in general. Who would have thought when she went through such pain and torment as a child and during her teenage years that just a few years into her twenties, she would be a popular and successful musician, an actor and television presenter, and a much-loved judge on Britain's leading talent show? So many hurdles and obstacles had been placed in her way, but Tulisa had found a way to overcome them all. So while she did feel stressed and tired by the demands of *The X Factor*, she was also able to keep them in perspective rather better than her rival judges, whose lives had not been as tough as hers. Could the tough and at times cold resolve that life had installed in Tulisa be her hidden weapon as the finishing line was in sight?

She gave her girls a final pre-show push by predicting that they would not just be a successful pop act but actually a force for good in British society in general. 'I think the thing about these girls, if they got that record deal and came out into this industry, they wouldn't just bring music to the UK, they would be inspiring lots of women across the country,' she said, in full-on electioneering mode. 'I think they would make a difference to people's lives as well as their ears.' she added. This had been a selling point that Tulisa had worked well during the live shows. Aware that girl bands often fail to attract votes from *The X Factor*'s largely female voting base, she approached the issue bravely by appealing straight to the hearts of female viewers. In doing so, she was positioning her band not as the next Saturdays, but the next Spice Girls – a movement and almost political brand as much as a pop band. As such, they were the perfect vessel to attract votes. Why vote for someone just because of how they sing and look, when you can also vote for them because they stand for something that connects with you? Having attached such a powerful message to her band, Tulisa could approach the final with confidence that she had given them the best chance possible. Just one more weekend of *X Factor* duty and she could finally take that well-earned holiday.

The moment Tulisa appeared on screen on the Saturday evening she captured the imagination of viewers. Indeed, her outfits for the two shows certainly got tongues wagging. On the Saturday, she emerged wearing a corseted mini-dress with a huge skirt, black netting, polka dots and layers of tulle. As a *Grazia* writer commented: 'Blimey...she ended up looking like a puffy cupcake, no?' She introduced her act three times on the Saturday show. At times during her introductions she seemed subdued, even depressed. Was it the pressure of the evening affecting her, or could it have been the words of Barlow, who while praising his own act had taken a thinly veiled dig at Tulisa. His reference to how often his rival judges had asked the public to vote for their respective acts, and to 'thumping of the table', seemed to unsettle Tulisa for a while. Big rows between judges during the final are often frowned upon by the public. Therefore, while she could undoubtedly have bitten back hard at Barlow, she did not.

She might have been subdued at times on the panel but when it came to her duet with her act, Tulisa was in strong voice. They performed a superb mash-up of Alicia Keys' 'Empire State Of Mind' and 'If I Ain't Got You'. She slotted into the line-up in the perfect way for the context: she seemed simultaneously at one with the band but with an element of elder stature. More than anything, her vocals were the best of the three judges in the eyes of many viewers. Twitter became awash with admiring comments from *X Factor* viewers, many of who seemed surprised that Tulisa had such great pipes. As she sang with her finalists, Tulisa seemed a million miles from the days when her *X Factor* role had first been revealed. Asked which of the three mentor-act duets he enjoyed most, Walsh particularly praised Tulisa's vocals with Little Mix. 'Honestly, I really liked all three,' he said of the duets. 'I love the bond between Gary and Marcus. But then the little muffin and the other little muffins came on! I didn't know Tulisa could sing that good,' he added.

During the sister show *The Xtra Factor*, the boss of the show finally made an appearance – albeit via satellite. Wearing sunglasses and sitting outside in a t-shirt, Simon Cowell was clearly enjoying being able to show the contrast between the weather on the west coast of America and that in London. He spoke admiringly of the final. 'Do you know what, it really made me miss being back in

Britain,' he said. 'It was absolutely amazing, one of the best finals I've ever seen and I wasn't on it.' Asked who he thought had performed best, he immediately chose Tulisa's act. 'No question, Little Mix won the night,' he said. 'I thought all three contestants did really well… but I got to say Little Mix are a revelation and if a girl group was to win the show, it makes history and maybe something special is going to happen.' He then turned to the criticism Tulisa and the rest of the panel had faced in the new series of the show. 'They've been great, the new panel this year,' he said. 'I've really enjoyed the show. [It] could have had a bit more controversy, but at the end of the day, it's all about finding stars, and I think tomorrow night Marcus versus Little Mix is going to be sensational… I couldn't call it.' However, he had clearly leaned more to Tulisa's act. Roll on Sunday.

On the Sunday Tulisa wore another eye-catching dress. This time it was a striking, full-length, mermaid-style gown. It had been made especially for her by Fyodor Golan, the winner of the 2011 Fashion Fringe. She seemed to have difficulty walking in the frock and needed to hold onto Louis Walsh's hand in order to reach the judges' panel without falling. Walsh looked a touch comical himself, wearing a bright red suit that resembled at first glance the sort of dressing gown one might imagine a 'young-at-heart' chum of Hugh Hefner to ill-advisedly sport at a *Playboy* mansion bash. Tulisa's final weekend outfits seemed to get the thumbs-down from many viewers. The following morning the *Daily Mail* opined that she had lost her overall 'style war' battle with Kelly Rowland. Her bold choices for the final weekend had certainly swung the newspaper's approval from her.

As for her act, they performed the Christmas carol 'Silent Night', En Vogue's 'Don't Let Go (Love)' and the winners' single, Damien Rice's 'Cannonball'. Marcus Collins, too, performed 'Cannonball' as his potential winners' single, but he seemed less comfortable with the track. Tulisa's act received wonderful feedback all night. Walsh said: 'I'm going to predict – Little Mix – big future.' Even Barlow – whose act was up against the girls – said: 'Simple, beautiful, emotional, very very Christmassy...Well done.' Tulisa said: 'Girls, I've pretty much said all I can say but I want to say to you again how proud of you I am from the bottom of my heart. You have done so well.' She then ramped up the emotion and gravitas in her voice, asking: 'And who said that a group can't win? Who said that a girl group can't win *The X Factor*? I believe you can do it and I hope you believe as well and I hope the UK believes you can do it – and I hope they pick up the phone and vote!' O'Leary said: 'She's at it again – she's like Winston Churchill or something.'

After they sang 'Don't Let Go (Love)', Barlow said, 'This is definitely your direction – great performance tonight. Well done.' Tulisa returned to her bombastic electioneering when she thanked viewers who had voted for Little Mix each week, and added: 'But why did you pick up the phone? You picked up the phone because you wanted them to get through and to get to the final and you wanted them to win this competition. So, those votes meant nothing unless you pick up the phone today, tonight, right now – they need it, it's the final. I'll say it again: they're not safe, so vote for Little Mix!' This time, O'Leary said: 'Oh man, I love it when Tulisa goes Jerry Maguire!'

After Little Mix had sung'Cannonball', it was time for each of the judges to have their final say . Summing up the mood of the moment, Walsh told Tulisa's band: 'The reason we're getting emotional is that four little pop princesses have been born.' Rowland said: 'I'm so happy. I'm so proud of you – congratulations.' Barlow encouraged them to continue supporting one another, as he predicted they had big things ahead of them. Then it was time for the closing comment of their mentor and master electioneer Tulisa. She told each member of the band in turn what they meant to her: 'Jade, you are the most adorable person I have ever known, Jesy, you are inspiring, Leigh-Anne, you remind me of myself years ago and Perrie, you were born a star. I love all of you. It's out of our hands now. Let's hope the public have voted.'

Finally, Tulisa joined her band onstage to stand alongside Barlow and Collins, as O'Leary announced the winner of *The X Factor*. She and her band leapt for joy when he revealed Little Mix had won. Leigh-Anne said: 'Oh my gosh, wow.' As the stunned excitement of the band became more palpable, sweet Jade said: 'I'm so grateful. Thank you for everybody who voted.' Perrie added: 'Oh my gosh, that's insane.' Only Jesy was able to speak more than a few words. She said: 'Oh my God, this is never going to sink in. We can't thank the public enough for picking up the phone.' Runner-up Collins was disappointed with coming second but his friendly and sporting side was just as clear in defeat. 'The girls really deserve it,' he said. 'They are amazing. I'm really proud of myself. Thanks to everyone who voted.' As for Tulisa, she said: 'I think I wanted them to win more than they did.' It was meant in jest but there was some truth to it – she had been a gloriously competitive and dedicated mentor. Naturally, she was in triumphant mood into the night and was quickly talking about putative collaborations between herself and Little Mix. 'There have been talks about us performing together again,' she said. 'When I release my album we might re-record the song we did together and put it on my album.'

Looking to the future, she said: 'I am here whenever they want me to be, they're my new best mates. They won because they are the most beautiful, genuine, talented girls and I love them.' Tulisa celebrated their final victory in a style that was more N-Dubz than *X Factor*: with a kebab. In the early hours of Monday morning she Tweeted: 'what do ya do after ur act wins the xfactor?...go 2 ur local kebab shop of course, wooooiiiiii....LOVE U #LITTLEMIX keep it real' Meanwhile it emerged that Simon Cowell had hired Richard 'Biff' Stannard, the songwriter who helped the Spice Girls find fame, to create a hit for Tulisa's winners. Biff is pop song-writing royalty, and the man who wrote the Spice Girls' debut smash hit 'Wannabe', the song that launched not just their musical career but their entire 'girl power' brand. More recently he has worked with the 2010 *X Factor* winner, Matt Cardle.

Tulisa said later she was attracted to the idea of managing Little Mix, but added that she believed this was not permitted. 'I would manage them if I was allowed to, but I guess that's not how it works,' she told Olly Murs and Caroline Flack on *The Xtra Factor*. 'I'm a mentor and I'm still going to be their mentor. I'm always going to be there for them. I will get involved as much as I can, as much as the label want me to be involved with them. I'm just gonna go with the flow and give them as much advice and help as I physically can.'

Interestingly, when the week-by-week voting statistics were released after the final vote had been announced, it showed that Little Mix had entered the lead only in the closing weeks of the race. The act that had finished top most often was Janet Devlin. She finished top in the first four weeks of live shows in which a public vote had taken place. Little Mix had first finished in the top two of the voting results in week four, when they came second to Devlin. They returned to the second place in week eight, and then for weeks 10 and 11 (the semi-final and final) they finished top of the voting.

For many, the true winner of the series had been Tulisa. She became the toast of the *X Factor* nation. The *Sun* claimed she had not only been guaranteed a place at the table for the 2012 series, but that she had been offered a doubling of her reported £450,000 salary to return. Interestingly, the unnamed source quoted in the *Sun*'s story claimed that, far from harming her popularity with the show's bosses, her clash with Misha B had actually been seen as a positive. It was said they admired her for sticking to her guns over the issue. While the veracity of the *Sun*'s claims has yet to be established, the *Sunday Mirror* quoted Tulisa as saying that she would be seeking a decent deal to return for the 2012 series. 'I definitely want to come back next series,' she was quoted as saying. 'But would I do it for a pay-cut? Definitely not. That's ridiculous.' Confident words, particularly in times of financial austerity.

She also wondered whether she would be able to create such a favourable rapport with her assigned category again. 'I do wonder if I'd get on with my contestants as well. It might have been first time lucky,' she reflected. In another development, she corroborated the perception that she was standing by her criticisms of Misha B. 'I never go back on my actions,' she said. 'For me it's about what happens behind the scenes as well as on stage,' she added. 'I wasn't lying. It was affecting one of my acts and the week something was said it stopped. I think even from Misha's point of view it is something she might not have realised she was doing. We had a talk and I think she's a lovely girl.'

Finally, it was time for her to return from planet *X Factor* to the real world as she moved to capitalise on her massive profile. It was a triumphant and confident return.

CHAPTER
ELEVEN

Suddenly, it seemed, lots of people wanted to collaborate with Tulisa. So successful and popular had she become, that people were keen to try and link up with her. Jessie J, who had assisted her at judges' houses, expressed a hope that they would record a song together. 'I'd love to do a track with Tulisa,' she said. 'We've talked about writing a song like "Do It Like A Dude" together. A big girl power anthem because we are both feminists.' Her praise of Tulisa took a saucy turn when she added: 'I popped in to see her in her *X Factor* dressing room for two minutes and ended up staying for two hours. We just get on really well and have such a laugh, plus she's got a great bum, which is fine with me.'

Tulisa was so happy in the wake of her X *Factor* commitments. The gamble had paid off and she couldn't stop smiling. 'When anyone asks me how I am, I go:

"Apparently I'm having a breakdown." That's a joke,' she said. She added: 'I was in Tesco and saw this headline saying: TULISA CAN'T TAKE IT ANYMORE! But here I am, strolling around the supermarket. Another story said my boyfriend was going to break up with me before Christmas. It's all made up.'

Having been in the *X Factor* bubble for months Tulisa was thrust back to N-Dubz matters when her two band-mates made significant statements in the immediate aftermath of her talent show involvement coming to a close. Talking about the *Greatest Hits* album, which he described as the 'golden jubilee' of the band's career, Fazer seemed to want to draw a line under the band's history to date. 'We've done three great albums but we're bored of performing these old songs now,' he told *Now* magazine. 'We want new material, so we're putting the old ones to sleep. Everything from 2012 on is a new chapter.' Then it emerged that during a solo concert by Dappy in Manchester just hours after Tulisa's *X Factor* victory, he had slated *The X Factor* to his audience. 'This is what fame is, not standing for hours outside to audition for *X Factor*,' he told the audience as he introduced the song 'Rockstar', which features Queen guitarist Brian May on its soundtrack. He then went one step further, shouting: 'F*** Simon Cowell!' His outburst drew some cheers from the audience but they were replaced with jeers when Dappy called a close to his set after scarcely 25 minutes.

The following evening Tulisa went to the *X Factor* 'wrap' party with Fazer. The annual bash has become a key part of the *X Factor* experience. The team let their collective hair down and party into the night. In 2011 it was held at the DSTRKT club in London. She looked magnificent in her figure-hugging, one-shoulder gold dress. The sparkly outfit made the most of her superb curves. Fazer wore a black suit and arrived wearing sunglasses, despite the late hour. Tulisa got into a misunderstanding with paparazzi upon their arrival. She later Tweeted that it was not a drunken row: 'believe me I wish I'd had more 2 drink after that!#toosober'. Someone who might have benefited from being a little more sober was the series bad boy Frankie Cocozza. Outside the bash Cocozza somehow became embroiled in an argument with a group of girls. As a photographer appeared on the scene there were unseemly scraps and squabbles. Fellow contestant Jonjo Kerr leapt into action and appeared to lash out in the direction of the photographer. Kerr, a former infantry solider, was joined in his protection of Cocozza by Nu Vibe's Bradley Johnson. It seemed that all ended well, as Cocozza and Kerr were spotted leaving a hotel the following morning trailed by two young women.

Tulisa, meanwhile, was back home and dreaming about her forthcoming holiday. According to the *Sun*, she planned to take some friends on the trip with her. 'Tulisa has had hardly any time to see her friends since she's been on the show,' said a source. 'This is her first time off in months and she can't wait to catch up with everyone properly.' The headline for the *Sun*'s story was a bit of a giggle: LA ISLA TULISA. Not that she was about to take her foot off the gas for long. As she told *Now* magazine's Dan Wootton: 'I always have to be doing something or I'd get bored. If I didn't have a career outside of being a judge, I'd be finished. I love being at home, but only for a certain period of time. I'm looking forward to getting into the studio to start my solo album.'

Tulisa's act Little Mix had been mostly conspicuous by their absence at the *X Factor* wrap party. Only Leigh-Anne had looked in briefly. Their mentor had something a bit special lined up for them for later in the week. Together with *Glamour* magazine, she treated them to a celebratory dinner party. Tulisa looked sensational as she arrived dressed in dramatic black. Among the guests was one of the band members' idols, former Spice Girl Emma Bunton, aka Baby Spice. Geri Halliwell, aka Ginger Spice, sent a bouquet of flowers to the girls. The event was held at the Roof Gardens venue in Kensington. After the dinner, Tulisa told her Twitter followers: 'So lovely to see Little Mix, it's all just starting for them! Such sweethearts!!!!' The following morning the band sent their own message to Twitter, writing: 'Went for dinner last nite with tulisa n glamour magazine was amazing! Also met Emma bunton wat an inspiration!'

In the final analysis, the only disappointment about Tulisa's first year as an *X Factor* judge is that she had not been a more feisty character onscreen. Asked what happened to 'the feisty Tulisa', she replied: 'She's still there.' Perhaps if she returns to the judging panel she will feel more confident to let the feisty Tulisa out to play a bit more. Here's hoping. The experience had certainly matured her as a person. The increase in scrutiny and criticism that all judges face had thickened her skin and broadened her perspective. 'I can't send a Tweet every time someone's abusive to me,' she said. 'I can't fight the world. I'm not bothered any more – I let it go over my head.' She looked ahead to 2012, a year in which the world had long been rumoured by some doom-merchants to end. For Tulisa, it is as if her life is only just beginning. With plans for a number of projects including a possible novel, autobiography and a solo career, she has much to be excited about. The 'Earthquake' rapper Labrinth is among those who are queuing to work with her. 'It's to be confirmed. It might happen,' he said. 'We did have talks about working on her record, and I would love to work with her so it might just happen anyway.'

As her fame and popularity rockets, Tulisa is keen to keep perceptions of her in proportion. She is not the first celebrity to profess distaste at the level of influence and respect they have accrued. In many cases, these protestations seem more than a little insincere – the disingenuous ramblings of people who complain about how famous and respected they are merely a way of reminding us how famous and respected they are. Such utterances are made during interviews whose sole attraction for the celebrity concerned is as a vehicle for boosting ever further the fame with which, they claim with a straight face, to be uneasy. As we have seen, Tulisa is not without contradictions, as evinced by her revised feelings about *The X Factor* following her invitation to join, yet she has certainly asked for people not to overestimate her worth. 'Just because I'm talented and I can write good music, it doesn't mean that I should be looked at as "wow" any more than you should, because it doesn't make a difference,' she said in 2010. 'Who cares? There's so much more going on in the world. There's kids starving in Africa and we're sitting there glitzing up on the red carpet.'

Perhaps having worked so hard to become as famous as she is, Tulisa can take a more considered look at the nature of the beast. Those who are catapulted to fame cannot, in all honesty, enjoy or understand the ride in the same way as someone like Tulisa. The legacy of her tough childhood continues to cast a shadow over her thoughts on her success. She admits that she has regular moments of doubts over whether she deserves her success. 'I'll think, "I don't belong here,"' she said. 'I get those moments now and again. I can be very feisty, but that's a defence mechanism for me. I'm defensive because too many years of my life I was treated like s***.'

When she was named *Now* magazine's 'Woman Of The Year' for 2011, she spoke about how her confidence has risen since becoming involved with *The X Factor*. 'I've become my own woman, not "'the N-Dubz bird",' she said. 'Getting away from the band and finding out what I want to do has given me confidence. You know how I used to spend so much time stressing? Now I can enjoy life.' However, while appreciating the confidence her new role had given her, she also explained that her experiences with N-Dubz had been useful. 'One thing I can say about N-Dubz is that it prepared me for being an *X Factor* judge,' she explained. 'N-Dubz was just as stressful – there were dramas every day. So I can sleep at night and I can handle it.'

Indeed, she felt that coming from a rough-and-ready, incident-fuelled band meant she found it easier to survive in the turmoil of *The X Factor* than the 2011 head judge did. 'I think it's harder for Gary because he's been a golden boy in the public and now he's got people criticising him for who he is,' she said. 'I've had criticism all my life, so it was nothing new to me.' Certainly Barlow had seemed to be displaying very mixed feelings about the experience. He seemed to buckle under the weight of public criticism and several times seemed upset and outraged when he was booed and heckled by the studio audience during the live shows. For Tulisa such treatment was easier to face. Compared to some of the controversy she had been flung into as a member of N-Dubz, the largely pantomime, storm-in-a-tea-cup hullabaloos of planet *X Factor* were definitely bearable.

In the final analysis, of the four judges Tulisa had thrived best. As we have seen, Barlow seemed uncomfortable at times. Also, his pronouncements that *The X Factor* was a 'singing contest' and that he wanted to find someone with 'real talent' were contradicted by his championing of the much-discussed Frankie Cocozza. Acts with undoubted superior vocal talent were dismissed by Barlow at both the judges' houses stage and in the first week of the live shows. Also, his criticism of Walsh for championing slightly novelty acts seemed hypocritical given his own support for Cocozza.

Rowland, meanwhile, started strongly but fell away the longer the series went on. Originally, her all-American patter was a breath of fresh air. She had a strong, definite personality, oodles of charisma and her glamorous looks went down a treat with male viewers. However, as the live shows progressed her persona seemed limited. She began to come across as a one-trick pony. Also, her rocky relationship with the generally admired and oft-loved Louis Walsh made her seem disrespectful to one of the show's key figures.

The aforementioned Walsh was his usual loveable Irish self for the most part but at times there were hints that he was uncomfortable in the new panel. His long-time friend Simon Cowell had gone, Rowland and Barlow were far from respectful to him, prompting him to remind them with genuine fury that he had 'been on the show for eight years'. Also, he was given the least promising category and did indeed lose all his acts quickly. This left him as a 'spare judge' while the other three continued to be contenders with acts in the competition. He looked a lost soul on the weekend of the final, often literally alone on the panel when the other three judges were tending to their acts.

As for Tulisa, she had none of the weaknesses of her fellow judges. Her approach and pronouncements were always perceived as honest and consistent. Her personality had stamina and her relationship with Walsh remained cordial throughout the series. She seemed absolutely dedicated to her acts. Indeed, her enthusiasm for all things *X Factor* came across throughout the run. Tulisa conducted herself as if she was born for *X Factor* and planned to hang around its environs for some years to come.

She had certainly endeared herself to Walsh. Their closeness was clear throughout the series and afterwards the Irishman spoke fondly of his fellow judge. His mixture of admiration and playful teasing suggested genuine warmth. 'We 100 per cent have a genuine friendship,' he said. He added that she is 'rough around the edges' and that was part of what he admired about her. 'You go into her dressing room and they're smoking and drinking.' He also said that her unpredictable nature was what he loved. 'She can be a bit of a loose cannon, but she cares,' he said. 'I love her honesty. What you see is what you get.' He added that he felt that Tulisa was the person involved with *The X Factor* that he felt he knew and understood best. That said, he said that sometimes she could be a know-it-all. Amusingly, he claimed ignorance of her band and indeed her career prior to *X Factor*. 'She talks about the N-Dubz like they're The Beatles but I didn't know who they were before the show,' said Walsh. 'I didn't know who she was either! Not everyone loves the N-Dubz – they're not the Black Eyed Peas. But I love her. And it's not a put-on thing for the cameras. I just can't do fake any more.' Well, how brave of you, Louis.

With Little Mix's debut single, 'Cannonball', going straight to No 1 in the UK charts, it seemed that Tulisa's first year as an *X Factor* judge was going to receive a fairytale ending. She said that for her, the chance to duet with Little Mix in the final had proved a vindicating climax to the experience. She had felt a suspicion from some over her qualification to judge a singing contest. However, she felt that her superb vocal performance in the duet with Little Mix, during which she outshone Barlow and Rowland's equivalent duets, proved her worth. 'Performing on the show was a big deal for me and I'm glad I nailed it,' she said. 'I felt like throughout the series I was continually having to prove myself as a judge. I had to justify why I was there in a way, even during the final. So actually being able to sing live with the girls in the final was a massive deal for me as well as them. People finally got to see that I wasn't just some street rat girl from N-Dubz who didn't have any talent. I got to show them what I was made of.'

She reiterated her desire to return as a judge when she said: 'I will be back if I'm asked but I haven't heard anything either way yet. I've loved working with the panel. Gary very sweetly sent me a bunch of flowers as a congratulations message [after the final], which I thought was a very noble thing to do.' The fact she had not been told whether she would be invited for the 2012 series was no surprise. Cowell and the *X Factor* producers like to keep their options open every year. They consider the fact that the judges are kept on tenterhooks keeps them fresh and keen. The uncertainty over the 2012 series went far beyond the question of Tulisa's involvement. A number of options were being considered, including delaying the start of the new series until early 2013, to allow the show a time to rest and to permit the return of Simon Cowell, who would by then be free of *X Factor USA* commitments.

However, Tulisa's narratives rarely conclude smoothly and she was not entirely playing ball with the *X Factor* brand. She was seen as taking a swipe at Little Mix's first single when she said: 'If I'm being honest the debut single "Cannonball" is more of a formality for them. The real fun will begin when they get in the studio and find their identity.' In fairness to Tulisa, the winners' singles of *X Factor* champions are rarely indicative of their broader career. Leona Lewis sang the cheesy ballad 'A Moment Like This' in the immediate wake of her victory, only to return the following year with the more credible 'Bleeding Love'. It was the latter single that set the tone for her career – 'A Moment Like This' was merely an immediate, if triumphantly sung, cash-in. Lewis would consider that the 'real fun' began for her with 'Bleeding Love'.

Some famous names have praised Little Mix – and not always the names one might expect. Despite his unease at the *X Factor* machine in general, Dappy said that for him the highlight of 2011 was when his cousin Tulisa's act Little Mix won the show. Indeed, he has taken a shine to some of the members of the band. 'I like Little Mix but I haven't met them yet,' he said in the wake of the show. 'They are very pretty, so they don't let me get too close to them.' So they at least had his seal of approval. There have been discussions that both Tulisa and her friend – and judges' houses sidekick – Jessie J would feature on the debut Little Mix album. 'It is not yet known how they will feature but it's likely they will appear on separate tracks,' a mole told the *Daily Star*. 'There was talk of forming a supergroup for one song but that got scrapped because Tulisa and Jessie are planning their own duet as well.'

****

While Tulisa has ratcheted up her celebrity in 2012, do not be surprised if she voluntarily steps away from show business within the next 10 years. She is certainly not inclined to become one of those celebrities who refuse to accept when their time is up and instead continue to chase fame with ever-decreasing reserves of dignity. Plus, she wants to focus on starting a family and cannot see that being easy to maintain alongside her career. 'It's too much,' she said. 'It's not the real world. I want to be able to have enough money to set up a future for my family. I want a business, something for my children. I want to get to my peak, and when I get to my peak, I want to go out with a bang.'

The mother hen of N-Dubz definitely wants to become a real-life mother in time. In fact, Fazer, speaking at the end of 2011, said that children could come sooner rather than later for the couple. 'We'll definitely have kids one day,' he began. 'I've always wanted children for as long as I can remember. You can just imagine them running around your feet like Mini-Me's.' They were even rehearsing for parenthood by sometimes looking after Milo and Gino, the kids of their band-mate Dappy. 'It's great because…we can just play with them then give them back when they get a bit annoying,' he said, speaking words that uncles, aunts, godparents and childless friends of young parents can relate to with a smile. 'It's definitely something I want one day, though.'

In the winter of 2011-12, Tulisa went on holiday. Inevitably, her figure was much commented on in the press, but fortunately she didn't have to try too hard to maintain it. 'I swear to God I don't do any exercise,' she said. 'I don't have a diet, I eat whatever I want. I love pizza and my nan's cooking. Even though I'm skinny, because of my lack of exercise, if you were to prod me you'd know I'm pure jelly. There's not an ounce of muscle on me. I like my legs – they're not long, but they look long against my body. When I wear heels, it seems like I've got long legs, but I'm only 5 foot 6 inches.'

It was also to be a trip during which she and Fazer finally began to show affection to one another in public. They stayed at the Coco Palm resort in the Maldives. She was seen wearing a printed string Lipsy bikini, while Fazer wore low-slung shorts over Calvin Klein underwear, a back-to-front baseball cap and some semi-bling jewellery as they strolled down the beach hand-in-hand. With her man in one hand and a cocktail in the other, Tulisa looked a million dollars and in paradise both physically and emotionally as she dipped her toes into the Indian Ocean. The couple were also seen frolicking in the sea. There could be no doubt they were an item – to borrow the tabloid cliché, they didn't mind who saw them together – and it was great to see them so happy together in such amazing surroundings. They split shortly after the holiday.

From an estimated £1,000-a-night holiday to the studio to work on the latest leg of her career – this sums up how life had turned out for our heroine. When Tulisa attempted suicide as a teenager this sort of life would have seemed unimaginable to her. Yet, through hard work and determination, she was now living the life of a top star. No more self-harming, bullying or poverty: thanks to her newfound riches and fame she had swapped vicious circles for exclusive ones. Even though Cowell refers to her as 'trouble', she now has a foot in his rich and exclusive world. So, what did she consider herself to be, socially, in 2012? Was she still the girl from the meaner streets of north London, or has she left that behind and become a middle-class luvvie? As far as Tulisa is concerned she was still the same girl that she always ways. Fame and fortune could never change that. Asked by a fan, 'Are you still a chav?' she said: 'Right, let's define "chav". Chav for me is a cockney. I'm a little bit cockney, a little bit urban, so…I really couldn't care what you call me. I'd say I'm from an urban, common area… I don't really give a shit what you want to call it. I'm the same person I was two years ago – if you want to call that a chav, good on ya.'

It seemed as if there were no clouds on the horizon, yet in March 2012 Tulisa found herself in the eye of the most contentious and sensitive media storm of her life when a tape, allegedly of her performing a sex act on a man, was published on the internet. The effect of the storm on Tulisa was almost devastating. 'I slept on the bathroom floor for seven days... I just wouldn't go out of the house,' she told the *Guardian*, in one of her first public utterances since the story broke. 'Couldn't sleep. Didn't really want to eat anything.' During that traumatic time she even, reportedly, considered leaving the country for good. Eventually, she 'snapped out of it'. Looking back, she felt that a period of torment was necessary for her to process her feelings. Only then, she believes, could she fully bounce back. 'I needed to have my tears and tantrums, my bad moods and get myself into a state to come back out of it,' she said. 'And I literally just woke up one morning, as happy as Larry, put on my best dress, make-up, full hair, "OK, I'm going out."'

With newspapers and magazines offering big bucks to Tulisa to comment, she uploaded a simply shot, five-minute statement onto YouTube. She said the fuss around the video had left her 'devastated' and 'heartbroken'. She insisted that she felt sure she should not be the one to 'take heat or stick' over the episode. Although she remained essentially composed throughout the video, the anger and hurt she felt over the episode was laid bare in a statement she submitted to the high court to support an injunction relating to the video. Her father, meanwhile, told the *Sunday Mirror* that what had happened had 'really brought the family down and destroyed us in some ways'.

Tulisa began to console herself with the knowledge that significant people in her life were backing her. For instance,

X Factor boss Simon Cowell declared, 'Tulisa doesn't have to apologise for anything.' There had been concerns that Cowell, perhaps fearful over a dent to *The X Factor*'s family image, might drop Tulisa over the episode. It was great news that this was not to be the case. Weeks later Cowell reaffirmed his faith in her when he said that as she 'won [*The X Factor*] last year, she is the reigning head judge.' He also invited her to perform as a guest act on *Britain's Got Talent*, an invitation she happily accepted.

By the first week of May, life had brightened for Tulisa as she was the subject of two bits of sensationally good news. On the Wednesday it was announced that she had received the much-coveted crown of *FHM*'s 'Sexiest Woman in the World' for 2012. Accepting it, she said: 'It's a true honour and definitely a lovely confidence boost. I'm proud of me and I am who I am. I know that I'm Marmite and I wouldn't wanna be anything less or anything more, I'm just myself.' That same week, on Sunday, she got the news she had dreamed of when her debut solo single, 'Young', went straight to UK No 1. Not only that, sales figures showed that 'Young' was the fastest-selling debut single of the year to date and the second fastest overall behind 'Hot Right Now' by DJ Fresh. It is richly deserving of such commercial success: it is a magnificent summer pop classic. Within hours of the summery song hitting No 1 she was confirmed for the Ibiza and Mallorca Live festivals.

Despite the success, some people will continue to call Tulisa all sorts of things and she will continue to do her best to accept that. She knows it comes with the territory.

While the horror with which some people greeted her appointment as an *X Factor* judge subsided once they saw the real Tulisa on their screens, for some she will always be a bit too wild and urban for them to truly consider her the nation's sweetheart, a position temporarily occupied by Cheryl Cole after she joined the show. However, one should recall that while Cole remains a working-class, Geordie celebrity, her past was never as wild as Tulisa's. In other words, she was closer to the rung of the ladder marked 'nation's sweetheart' before she set foot in the *X Factor* sphere. In fact, Tulisa is actually closer to being 'the people's princess', though not in the same way as Princess Diana – who earned that title via Tony Blair. Rather, Tulisa is the princess of the people who consider themselves *the* people. For them, any controversies surrounding their heroine are unlikely to shake their admiration for a girl who worked hard for her celebrity stature. Indeed, Tulisa did not want to become the second Cheryl but the first Tulisa.

After her own tumultuous childhood had tested Tulisa to the hilt, she will want to be a perfect mother to her own kids. She continues to develop her faith, too. Even before she goes onstage she takes a few moments to say one Hail Mary, one Our Father and then adds: 'Thank you, God, please give me the strength to tear up this show.' This is just one of the many things that we have found about her in these pages that confound the majority of the public's perception of her. It is important to share the real Tulisa, so more people can be inspired by her. As well as her explicitly religious moments, a more everyday personal philosophy for life she has outlined is: 'You only live once and the main thing in life is to be positive, do the best you can and try to be happy. No matter where you are or what you are doing, there's no point in anything unless you are happy.' After the challenges life has thrown at her she could only have thrived by adopting and sticking with such an approach.

What would the shy, geeky Tula Paulinea Contostavlos, standing alone in the playground at La Sainte Union school, have made of the conquering goddess she would blossom into? She is surely a person her younger self could be proud of. The story so far ends on a note of faith and promise, with Tulisa looking to the future. 'I'm a lot more religious now,' she said in May 2012. 'I kind of stopped believing in God but as I got older I found my faith again – and with that has come morals. My naughty days are firmly in the past.'

BIBLIOGRAPHY

Linda Blair, *Birth Order*, Piaktus, 2011
N-Dubz, *Against All Odds: from Street Life to Chart Life*,
Harper Collins, 2010

ACKNOWLEDGEMENTS

Thanks to: Lucian Randall, Joanna Kennedy, John Blake, Michelle Signore and Chris Morris. Thanks also to my mother, for her amusing voicemail message asking, 'How is your Turlooloo book coming along?'

Chas Newkey-Burden is a leading celebrity biographer whose subjects include Amy Winehouse, Simon Cowell, Brangelina, Tom Daley and Stephenie Meyer. His books have been translated into 14 languages. He has also co-written books with Kelvin MacKenzie and Julie Burchill. He is a regular guest on BBC Radio London and a columnist for the *Jewish Chronicle*.

Follow him on Twitter: @AllThatChas